To: Deb
Good Luck yo
Elson Buck SEE

An Uncommon Man:
Elson "Buck" See

Larry See

Headline Books, Inc.
Terra Alta, Wv

An Uncommon Man: Elson "Buck" See

by Larry See

copyright ©2014 Larry See

To order additional copies of this book or for book publishing information, or to contact the author:

Headline Books, Inc.
P.O. Box 52
Terra Alta, WV 26764
www.headlinebooks.com

Tel. 800-570-5951
Email: mybook@headlinebooks.com

ISBN 13: 978-0-938467-78-6

Library of Congress Control Number: 2013944927

PRINTED IN THE UNITED STATES OF AMERICA

To my Dad
and all of us who love
this Uncommon Man.

1

My father's name is Elson Markwood See, but he was given the nickname Buck at an early age, so I grew up being called, "Buck See's Baby." His story begins before the turn of the century. I don't mean the 21st Century, but rather the 20th Century. In 1891 his father, Homer See, was born in an area called Sulphur Springs near the tiny rural village of Old Fields in Hardy County, West Virginia.

Old Fields is situated five miles north of Moorefield, the county seat of Hardy County, and is located in the heart of the South Branch of the Potomac River Valley, an area with broad, fertile farmland and dense forests. Homer grew up as a logger who cut and hauled mine props to various coalmines in the George's Creek area of Western Maryland, near Cumberland. Once he started a family of his own, he became a farmer and remained one for the entire 84 years of his life.

Dad's mother, Emily Martin See, was born in that same year in another rural community called Cabin Run, which is situated just off Route 46 near Fort Ashby in Mineral County. She and Homer were married in 1914 and started a family that grew to nine children. As a farmer's wife, Emily took care of the house and the children who were not yet old enough to work outside in the fields, prepared all the meals on a wood-burning cook stove, and canned tons of vegetables from the garden for winter consumption by her large family.

The life of the See family was hard and filled with many sorrows, but an equal number of joys. Their family, which consisted of five boys and four girls, lived off the land on two rural farms in Hampshire County, West Virginia, and survived through the Great Depression and World War II. Homer and Emily witnessed the deaths of three of their children and three of their sons-in-law, but they persisted through faith in the Lord and in each other.

But I'm not the one qualified to tell about Homer and Emily. I didn't come along until 1954, and by that time they were older, and all their children were grown and raising families of their own. In fact, the sole person qualified to tell about my grandparents and my father's life is Buck See himself. After all, this is his story.

Part One:
Childhood

2

I was born on February 9, 1924, in a small farm-house near Rada, West Virginia. For those of you not familiar with the landscape of rural Hampshire County, Rada is a tiny settlement on West Virginia Route 220, midway between Romney and Moorefield. Actually, our home place was located at the foot of a ridge called Pine Log, a short but steep incline on the road to Chert Mountain, site of an apple orchard that at one time was the largest individually owned orchard in the entire country.

I lived on this farm with my mother, father, and seven brothers and sisters. I was the sixth child and third son born to Homer and Emily See. My oldest brother was Eldon, and he was followed into this world by my two sisters, Hazel and Lessie. Then came my brother Ellis and my third sister Virginia. After my birth came James and Esther. Our final sibling was a boy who died only two days into his life from some type of birth defect that was never really explained to me.

As if our house wasn't crowded enough, my Grandmother Martin lived with us for over a year during my childhood. She fell and broke her hip, and after an extended stay in the hospital, she couldn't care for herself well enough to live on her own, so we took her in. Family bonds were the strongest at that time, and despite the cramped conditions, we cared for her in our home until she passed away.

My childhood was filled with many hours of work and play on the two farms that we owned. From as far back as I can remember, I milked cows, fed chickens, slopped hogs, and pulled weeds in the garden, the same chores that all children on all small family farms across the country performed. We lived a hard life, but it was a good life, filled with work, family, and friends.

My oldest brother Eldon tired of this simple life and struck out on his own when I was fourteen. He had been driving a truck for my father up to that point. Daddy had been awarded a contract to haul coal from the mines on the Allegany Front to the tannery in Moorefield. Eldon made two trips per day from the mines to the tannery, but after a couple of years my father lost the contract to a lower bidder. Employment was scarce in the mid 1930's at the height of the Depression, but Eldon then landed a job with a man named Tom Gulick, who lived just east of Romney, up a hollow behind the old Sanders Tavern.

Eldon drove a truck for Mr. Gulick, and each morning he would drive to the mines in the George's Creek vicinity to pick up a load of coal that he would then haul to residents in the Washington, D.C. area to be used to heat their homes. He stayed in the Gulick home to save money on rent, and although he was far from rich, he was able to scrape by on the few dollars that Mr. Gulick paid him for each load he hauled.

One evening after work, Eldon stopped by Sanders

Tavern for a drink. As often happened in beer joints (that's what taverns were called in our part of the country), an argument between Eldon and another patron broke out and then escalated into a fistfight. In the melee, the other man grabbed a beer bottle and hit Eldon over the head with it, knocking him unconscious.

After several minutes, Mr. Gulick finally revived Eldon and took him home. He called a doctor, who came to the house and wrapped up the nasty gash on Eldon's head and told him to lay off work for a few days until he felt better. But Eldon never did feel better. He remained in a semi-conscious state for the better part of three weeks, but for some reason Mr. Gulick never felt compelled to contact either a doctor or my parents, who had no idea that anything had even happened to their son.

Finally, Mr. Gulick made a trip to our farm in Rada and told Mother and Daddy about Eldon's condition. They drove to Romney to see him and instantly sensed the gravity of his condition. They took Eldon to the hospital in Keyser, a trip of about 25 miles, where he stayed for a week before he passed away from spinal meningitis, which he contracted as a result of the head wound. Eldon was only twenty-four years old when he died, his whole life still ahead of him. Grief gripped our house and lives for months and even years after the loss of our eldest sibling.

No charges were ever filed against the man responsible for Eldon's death. I've often wondered why Tom Gulick waited so long before telling my parents about Eldon's condition. I suppose he felt that Eldon's injuries weren't that serious, and that he would start to improve any day. If we could have gotten him to the hospital right after the accident, I can't help but feel that Eldon would have survived. But such were the harsh times we lived in during those days.

3

Our first farm contained 49 acres of fields and woodland. We had cows and chickens and hogs, so we never bought meat at the store. The same held true for vegetables. We had a huge garden that the whole family worked, and this garden provided fresh vegetables in the summer and fall and more than enough excess to can for eating in the winter and spring.

We planted a large patch of what my mother called soup beans. In the fall we would spend days picking these beans, which were encased in a hard shell. After we picked a bushel or so, we put them in a burlap sack and placed them flat on a table or even on the ground. We then beat the sack with a stick to hull out the beans, which we separated from the hulls when we poured them out of the sack. These beans made a hearty and delicious soup that heated up the family on cold winter days. Despite the hard times that the rest of the country was suffering through, I can't ever remember going hungry the whole time I was growing up.

Daddy owned a truck when we lived at the foot of Pine Log, and he made his living from that vehicle. He would cut mine props from the oaks and other hardwoods on our farm and haul them to the George's Creek area, for use in the many coalmines there. My father cut down the trees for the props with a cross-cut saw, since chainsaws had yet to be marketed in the U.S., and he trimmed the trees with a double-bit axe.

These props ranged in length from eight to sixteen feet and were five to six inches in diameter. Before we boys were big enough to be of assistance in this project, Daddy occasionally hired a man to help him cut and load these very heavy logs. This was backbreaking work with primitive tools, but as each of us boys matured we were able to help ease his burden.

We also had a small orchard with perhaps 150 to 175 peach, apple, and cherry trees that Daddy planted shortly after we moved to the farm. That may not sound like such a small orchard by today's standards, but when compared to the 1,000 acres in Leatherman's Orchard on Chert Mountain, ours was a tiny operation. The soil and climate were ideal for growing fruit in that area. We seldom had a late frost in the spring that would damage the buds on the fruit trees, I guess because the air always seemed to stir in the evening and early morning.

The orchard was a lot of work. We pruned the trees in the fall and thinned the crop in late spring. We had no pesticides to spray on the trees at that time, and I recall a certain worm that would bore into the roots of the peach trees and eventually kill them if not eliminated. We had to carefully dig down around the roots of the trees and cut out the worms. Again, this was boring, backbreaking work, but we had to do it to maintain our source of income.

Daddy would fill the truck with mine props, but he always left a little room on the back for several bushels of peaches, apples, and cherries in the fall of the year. When the harvest was at its peak, he would completely fill the truck with fruit and peddle it in Cumberland and the surrounding area. That orchard served us quite well the entire time we lived on that farm.

One late summer afternoon when I was eight or nine, a stranger pulled up to our house in a pick-up truck. Mother met him on the porch, and he told her that he had talked to my father that morning on one of his runs to deliver mine props to George's Creek. He said that he and Daddy had struck a deal whereby this man would pick up a load of peaches and deliver them to some of my father's regular customers. After he was paid for the delivery, the man would return to the farm and settle up payment for the fruit.

Not knowing exactly what to do but having no reason to doubt the man's word, Mother told us kids to go to the orchard and pick enough peaches to fill up the man's truck. After several hours, the man pulled away with a full load and headed toward Cumberland.

When Daddy returned home later that evening, Mother told him that we met the man he sent to the house to pick up the fruit, and that he left for Cumberland just as they had arranged. My father asked her what in the world she was talking about. Mother repeated the story, and Daddy said that he made no such deal with anyone. He asked if she had gotten the man's name, and Mother replied that she hadn't.

We'd never seen the man before or since, but we figured he had to be someone who either watched the house closely to determine when Daddy would be away, or he was an acquaintance of one of our neighbors who knew my father's work routine. Either way, he sure took a real dent out of our profits for that fall. This incident just shows how desperate some people were to survive during those hard economic times.

4

My father was always looking to expand his operation, so in 1934, right after I turned ten years old, he saw a notice in the Hampshire Review, the weekly newspaper in Hampshire County, that a 315-acre farm, which included a sizeable farmhouse and a store that housed the Rada Post Office, was going to be auctioned off on the steps of the courthouse in Romney. The First National Bank of Romney had foreclosed on the loan it made to a man named Charlie Davy, and the bank was selling the property to recover part or all of the remaining money on the loan. My father was determined to buy that farm.

On the scheduled day of the auction, Daddy drove to Romney and approached the auctioneer, who was a man that he knew from previous dealings. He casually asked the auctioneer how much he thought the land would sell for. Since he worked on commission, and he also felt a sense of duty to the bank, which had hired him, he told Daddy that he would try to squeeze every penny that he could out of the sale.

Daddy asked him what he thought about a $6,000 bid to start the proceedings. The auctioneer looked at him incredulously, but my father assured him that he could get the money and insisted that he start the bidding at that price. Thinking that to be a fair price even if no other bids were offered, the auctioneer agreed. I suspect that he also felt that if the bidding started at such a high figure, then there was no telling how high the price might go. All this negotiating was done behind the scenes while the other interested patrons filled in around the courthouse steps.

The appointed hour arrived, and the auctioneer walked out onto the steps to begin the sale. He told those assembled there that he had a bid of $6,000 to start the auction and asked if anyone wanted to bid higher. The crowd looked stunned as they scanned around for the rich man who had started the bidding so high. All the while my father stood silently at the rear of the crowd.

The auctioneer asked once more for a higher bid, but the crowd started to sense that he was just bluffing about the bid in order to jack the price up as much as possible. He once more asked for another bid, this time assuring the crowd that he intended to sell if no other bids were offered. He called once, twice, and three times with no results, and then he sold the property to my father.

Now $6,000 may not seem like such a large sum of money to pay for such a big piece of real estate today, but in 1934, at the height of the Depression, $6,000 was a lot of money. The 49-acre farm that we owned would fetch some of the money, but it had yet to be sold. Daddy was making a passable living from his truck and the orchard, but when he sold his present place the orchard would belong to the new owner, cutting his revenues considerably.

But my father had a good head for business, and he knew that the farm, along with the store and post office, was worth considerably more than he had paid for it. He just had to convince a bank to have faith that he could earn enough off the farm to make the payments.

Ironically enough, he got his loan from the First National Bank, the very institution that made the original loan. We moved to our new home, and Daddy began to pay off his debt.

He had made two or three payments when the bank apparently started to have second thoughts about the loan. Daddy had just made a payment at the bank when the president, a man named Marvin Williams, stopped him as he was leaving. He told my father that he needed to talk to him about his finances and wondered if he could drive out to the farm one evening to discuss the matter.

A couple of days later, Mr. Williams appeared at our door, and when he sat down in the living room he immediately started expressing his concerns. He said he couldn't pinpoint the exact cause, but he just felt that we were not going to be able to keep up with our payments, and that he was sure that foreclosure was in our future. Daddy asked him why he felt that way, since he had already made three payments, in full and on time. Mr. Williams said his experience in the banking field made him think that way.

My father said that this was a poor way to do business, since he should have voiced these concerns before the money was loaned. Daddy also said that since Mr. Williams had no faith that the loan would be repaid, then perhaps he should try to borrow money from another institution. Mr. Williams apologized for his feelings, but he didn't retract them before he left.

The following day my father gave up a day of work to travel to Romney to a firm called the Federal Land Bank of Baltimore, which was the predecessor of today's Farm Credit. He heard that the Federal Land Bank was willing to take a chance on financing small farms, and sure enough, the loan was secured that very day.

Daddy said that Mr. Williams nearly fainted when he showed up with a check for the entire amount of the loan and told him that his finances were no longer of any concern to Mr. Williams or his bank. My father was not only hard headed, but he was also a hard man with a dollar, a lesson he passed down to me and all his other children.

5

My education began in 1930 when my brothers and sisters and I would make the three-mile trek on foot from our farm to a one-room schoolhouse near a community called Russeldale to study under the watchful eye of one Marguerite Shoemaker, a redheaded terror who conducted her classes with an iron hand.

There were no buses at that time, so if kids wanted to attend school they had to walk there. And yes, it was uphill both ways. We followed a direct route across ridges, through fields, and past neighbors' houses, and I never seemed to mind the walk since I always had my brothers and sisters to keep me company.

After we moved to our new farm, I attended the Rada School, which was only about a quarter of a mile from our home. I even made a little money during my time at Rada School. The one-room school was heated by a big wood stove, which was located in the center of the room. In the winter, the board of education paid me $2.00 a month to fire that stove. I would arrive at school early, before the teacher or any of the students, and build a fire so the classroom would be warm when the others arrived. I didn't get rich, but every little bit helped.

I graduated from the eighth grade at age 14, but I was far too valuable on the farm to attend high school, which was located in Romney, eleven miles from my home. I learned to read and write and work out math problems in elementary school, and those were the only skills necessary for survival in our rural community at the time. My sisters Virginia and Esther were the only children in our family who were afforded the luxury of attending high school, but neither of them graduated.

Money was tight, and if we were going to keep and profit from our new farm, then everyone had to do his or her part. We each were assigned specific duties, aside from the normal chores like feeding and watering the animals and taking care of the house, which we all helped with. My job was to work with and care for the horses on the farm.

Mill Creek ran through the heart of our farm. It was a small stream, fifteen or twenty feet wide and anywhere from six inches to two feet deep, that never went dry, even in the hottest part of the summer. Beside the creek were our fields, which were the lifeblood of the farm. We had four different creekside fields, each of which contained from 10 to 30 acres. These fields had to be plowed in the spring in order to plant the corn, wheat, and oats that we used to feed not only the family but also the cattle and pigs and chickens that we used for food.

We couldn't afford a tractor or a big plow, so all the plowing was done with horses and a single-blade plow that turned over the dirt one row at a time. I was the one in charge of this project each spring. I would literally spend all day in the warm spring sunshine, crossing back and forth across those fields, breaking up the soil a single row at a time.

My day began at or near sunrise, and I worked until noon, when I returned to the house for lunch and fed and watered the horses. Afternoon would find me back behind the horses until my day ended near sundown. I was so tired when I finished caring for the horses that I could barely eat my supper before collapsing into bed, only to start the entire process over the next morning.

In the fall, we harvested our crops and stored them for the winter. We took our wheat to be ground into flour at a mill in Williamsport, a wide place in the road about five or six miles from our farm. The mill had a water wheel that was powered by a small creek that flowed out of the mountain. We had a hallway that led to the back part of our house, and that hallway was always crammed with 25-pound sacks of flour after we returned from the mill.

Such was life on nearly every small farm during the Depression. We had practically no money, except what my father made hauling props and selling some livestock, and what little money we had went toward the debt on the farm. We didn't buy any food at the store, at least not while we lived at the foot of Pine Log. I never tasted what we called "baker's bread," which was bread bought in a store, until we moved down to the new farm at Rada. And even then we didn't use money to buy supplies, but rather we traded eggs to the store for the few necessities that we had to have.

The Rada Store, which was part of the farm when we bought it, was another source of income. A man named Elmer May was running the store when we bought the farm, but he moved on shortly after that. We then rented the store to Lyle Cunningham, and the money he paid us each month out of his profits helped out with the farm payments. Mr. Cunningham also inherited the job of postmaster when he rented the store, which was a very good thing because Daddy was the postmaster before Mr. Cunningham, and he knew absolutely nothing about the job.

After Lyle Cunningham moved on, my sister Hazel and her husband Bill ran the store and the post office before my father eventually sold both to a man named Ed Everett, for a handsome profit I might add.

6

Despite our scarcity of money, Mother always put three hot meals on the table every day, and the food was filling, plentiful, and delicious. If nothing else, we had meat and potatoes and bread and milk, and with those staples around, if you left the table hungry then it was your own fault. I don't know how she did it, laboring over that hot stove, winter and summer. On the hottest days of the summer, it was sweltering inside her kitchen, with the windows open and prayers lifted for just a breath of air.

She baked bread and pies and cakes on that stove, and she seemed to know just how much wood to put in the stove and the exact spot on the top or in the oven to prepare each dish. We had buckwheat cakes just about every morning for breakfast. Mother saved what she called a starter from the previous day's batter, and then she added ingredients to make that morning's batter. The longer she carried over the batter, the more sour the buckwheat cakes would get. I can still remember the taste of those buckwheat cakes, which she prepared on a long griddle that held four or five cakes at a time. They were like no others I've had since, but a mother's cooking is always the best.

This was a time before television, but we did enjoy listening to the radio in the evenings. We heard a lot about the Depression, but I can honestly say that the financial troubles of the rest of the country had little or no impact on my childhood for several reasons. First of all, I'm not really sure that I realized that we were poor because every other family in our community was in the same boat. Nobody had much money, so we all pretty much dressed and acted alike.

We were also basically self-sufficient. We raised nearly all of our own food, and we had enough produce to trade or animals to sell to buy the seed and fence and other necessities that we had to have to keep the farm running.

But most of all, we were satisfied with what we had. We never had any luxuries in the house, so we didn't lose anything when the Depression hit. We were simple country folks that took care of our land and our family, and we were content with the essential things in life. We heard about the Stock Market Crash and the other distressing economic news at home and abroad, but we continued to function in our own little corner of the world, focusing on the things that were right before us and letting tomorrow take care of itself when the time came.

7

Our quality of life improved a great deal when we moved to the new farm at Rada. The house was much bigger and more suited to our large family. But there were also some conveniences that we had never experienced before.

The house had running water, even though we didn't have electricity or a pump. There was a cistern that had been dug in the hollow behind our house. The cistern was fed by a spring that never went dry. The spring even supplied a small run that flowed past our house. The previous family built a shelter to cover the cistern and ran galvanized pipe from the cistern to our house, thus giving the house running water. The system worked great for the first few years that we lived there, but eventually the pipes rusted and began to leak. The leaks became so bad that Daddy finally did away with the whole system and filled in the cistern with dirt to prevent a cow or other animal from falling into it and drowning.

We also had a refrigeration system that was efficient just about year round. There was a large icehouse located just off the kitchen. Its inside dimensions were

12'x 20', and it was nearly as tall as our house. It was constructed so the runoff water from the melting ice was funneled into a trough that ran along the front of the building. Mother would place all her perishables, like milk and cream and butter, in this water, which was cold even in the hottest part of the summer. The ice lasted well into the fall, so we had a refrigerator at our disposal almost all the time.

We couldn't afford to buy enough ice to fill up the icehouse, so we improvised. Patterson's Creek, a stream that was thirty to forty feet wide and seven or eight feet deep at its deepest point, was located about five or six miles from our farm, in Russeldale, the site of my first school. In December or January, after the weather had turned really cold, my father and we boys would hitch up the team of horses and pull our wagon to Patterson's Creek to get ice.

I'm not a big proponent of Global Warming, but it does seem to me that the winters were much colder when I was a boy. We usually got our first frost in September, and the weather pretty much stayed cold for the rest of the winter, with temperatures well below zero common during December, January, and February. The cold weather assured us that Patterson's Creek had frozen solid, and thus we were safe to get our ice.

We chopped out two-foot squares of ice with a broad axe, which had a wide, sharp bit that was perfect for chopping through the ice. It was common for the creek to freeze to a depth of a foot or two, which left a big, heavy chunk of ice to pull up out of the water. We used a set of metal tongs to pull the ice up, with a man or boy on each side to share the load.

We loaded these chunks on the wagon and hauled them back to the farm. We stacked the blocks of ice in the icehouse in layers, placing a coating of sawdust on each layer for insulation. We crammed in as many rows as the icehouse would hold, since we knew that the more ice we put in the icehouse the longer it would last into the next summer and fall. The ice never quite made it all the way to the next winter, but we were close enough that cooler weather had set in and the chance of perishables spoiling was greatly reduced.

Getting water became somewhat less convenient after our running-water system gave out. The previous owners of the farm dug a well by hand before the running-water system was completed, and we put that well to good use. The well was twenty-five feet deep and about four feet across. It had a roof over the opening that rested on four posts. We had a bucket attached to a rope on a crank, and we would lower the bucket into the well until it filled with water. We then cranked the bucket back up and emptied the water into another bucket, which we carried into the house.

The walls of the well were covered with rocks, and moss would form on these damp walls. Also, other dirt and mess would fall into the well and accumulate on the bottom. Once a year, usually in the summer, Daddy decided that the mess in the well had to be cleaned. I drew that assignment.

The water in the well wasn't all that deep, so the first step was to scoop out as much of the water as we could. I would then climb into the bucket and my father would crank me down into the well. I remember how cool and damp it was twenty-five feet below the ground as I scrubbed the walls and removed as many of the loose objects in the bottom as I could. I can't say that cleaning the well was fun, but it had to be done, so I did it.

We planted grape vines at the base of each post that held the roof over the well, and these vines spread until they covered the entire roof. My reward for cleaning the well was eating as many grapes as I could before Mother ran me off. She said that she needed those grapes to make jelly in the fall.

8

Money was always tight after we moved to the new farm at Rada, with those big mortgage payments hanging over our heads. When I got a little older, I decided to get a job to help bring in a little extra money. At that time the largest employer in our community was Chert Mountain Orchard.

The orchard was owned by Edgar Leatherman and covered 1,000 acres on the top of Chert Mountain. At that time, it was the largest orchard owned by one individual in the entire United States. Apple trees literally stretched as far as the eye could see on both sides of the top of the mountain. It took an army of people to keep the operation going. Mr. Leatherman owned several company houses in which most of his full-time employees lived, but the orchard also hired many seasonal workers, especially in the fall of the year at apple picking time.

The fall after I turned thirteen, when all the crops had been harvested and the farm had been prepared for winter, I went to the orchard to ask Mr. Leatherman for a job. He said that he could always use a good apple picker, and he told me to report for work the next morning.

There was a definite technique to picking apples. I was placed on the Red Delicious trees, some of which grew as tall as 30 or 40 feet. They were located on the side of one of the steepest hills in the orchard. We picked as many apples as we could reach from the lower and upper sides of the trees, and we had forty-foot ladders to reach the rest.

We carried a picking sack, which had a metal frame around the top with a canvas sack attached to the bottom and straps that went around your neck and over your shoulders. Each of these sacks held about a bushel of apples, and they were extremely awkward to handle while climbing up and down those ladders. I shoved the sack to my side as I climbed and then adjusted it back to the front when I started picking. A bushel of apples suspended in a sack hanging in front got really heavy, especially on those ladders.

When the sack got full, the pickers emptied it into bushel crates that were scattered liberally around the trees. We had to be extra careful when we handled the apples, especially when we were emptying our sacks into the crates, because we were paid less per bushel if a certain percentage of our apples had bruises, which were soft spots caused from dropping or rough handling.

We earned five cents a bushel if our apples were in prime condition, but the price could go as low as three cents a bushel if our apples had a lot of bruises. Each picker had stickers that he attached to the crates as he filled them, so he could get credit for each bushel he picked.

I was young and slim and strong, but I soon discovered that I would never become a good apple picker. I just never could get the hang of it. I worked hard every day, but I never seemed to improve. Our total output for the day was measured in barrels, which was the term they used for three bushels of apples.

I recall a young man by the name of John Dove who worked in the Red Delicious trees when I was there. He could climb up that ladder and around in those trees like a monkey. He commonly picked 100 barrels, or 300 bushels, in a day. That meant that he earned between $9 and $15 per day, not king's wages but a pretty fair paycheck for those days. My largest total ever was 35 barrels, or 105 bushels, in a day, which meant my highest daily pay was between $3.15 and $5.25, depending on the quality of the apples I picked. But a paycheck between $15 and $25 a week still helped out with the bills at home.

My father also worked on the orchard in the fall. He purchased two more trucks, which were stripped down models that were basically a motor and wheels with a bed behind, and landed a contract from Mr. Leatherman to haul the apples from the orchard to the packing shed.

As each picker filled a crate, he placed it along a road that ran between every four rows of trees. Daddy would drive along that road and load the crates onto his truck, with each truck holding 120 crates. Two men walked beside the truck to lift the crates up to the bed, and another worker rode on the back of the truck and stacked the crates. I soon discovered that I could make more money working on one of the trucks, and I changed to that job after just a few weeks.

I continued to split my labor between working on the farm and on the orchard until I turned seventeen. My younger brother James was old enough to take over some of my duties on the farm as he matured, so I went on the search for my first full-time job.

9

My brother-in-law Bill Shoemaker landed a job with the Baltimore and Ohio (B&O) Railroad in Keyser, a small town about 15 miles from our home, in Mineral County. He told me that the work was hard, but he also noted that the pay was good (ninety cents an hour, which was a great wage at that time), and they were hiring. I went to their office in Keyser to fill out an application, and a few days later they sent word home with Bill that I had been hired.

Bill sure wasn't kidding when he said the work was hard, and I got a good sample on the very first day of the type of backbreaking work I would be doing there. In the middle of the railroad yard stood a huge building called a round house. The round house contained a set of tracks mounted on a turntable. When a locomotive pulled onto the tracks, the turntable was rotated 180 degrees, allowing the locomotive to head in the opposite direction in preparation for its next load to pull.

The floor of the round house was dirt, and on my first day of work we determined to change it to concrete. The railroad owned a one-yard concrete mixer that was powered by a Model T engine. A worker would load the sand, gravel, and cement into the mixer with a shovel, and then he would add the proper amount of water. When the ingredients were blended into concrete, the finished mix was dumped into wheel barrels. My job, along with several other men, was to wheel this concrete into the round house and dump it on the floor.

I'm not sure if you're familiar with pouring concrete, but when it comes out of the mixer, it is wet and unstable and very heavy. It takes great strength and even better balance to push a wheel barrel full of concrete without slopping it all over the place. I struggled to keep up at first, but as the day wore on I improved quite a bit, and by the end of the day I was as good as any of the others on the project.

When quitting time rolled around at last, I was exhausted. I felt like a robot when I tried to roll out of bed for my second day of work. But my misery had just begun because it took about two months for us to complete the project. I can't say that I looked forward to work each morning until the concrete floor was in place.

When the floor in the roundhouse was completed, I was assigned to what was called a maintenance of way gang. This group included six workers, and our job was to repair and maintain ties, tracks, and bridges along the B&O lines. We traveled anywhere B&O tracks were laid, often going away for several days or weeks at a time. The railroad paid for our food and lodging while we were away from home on a job.

I recall that one of our first assignments was in Oakland, Maryland, a small town in the mountains of the western part of the state, about sixty miles from my home. We stayed there for three or four weeks installing warning poles for brakemen on the trains. These poles were placed alongside the track approximately 200 yards before a bridge or tunnel. A rope long enough to reach down to the top of the train was suspended from an arm on each pole.

The brakemen often worked and walked along the tops of the cars while the train was in motion, moving from car to car to draw the brakes on various parts of the train when necessary. When they saw or felt one of these warning ropes, they knew that low clearance was coming up shortly. They would then lie down on the top of the car, or they would crawl down between two cars until the danger passed.

Each morning the whole gang would cram into a speeder, a motorized car that had train wheels and ran on the rails, and travel several miles from Oakland to set a new pole or to make sure that an existing pole was stable and still had the warning rope attached.

We were basically on call twenty-four hours a day while we were away from home. One night we were sitting in our hotel room in Oakland playing cards before bedtime. The B&O tracks ran just a few feet from the door of the hotel. Railroad cars were equipped with what were called hot boxes, which were located close to the wheels and held lubricant to cool the wheels as the train rolled along. Apparently the hot box on one of the cars malfunctioned, and a wheel overheated and fell off, causing the car to derail. That car caused three others to derail before the train could stop, with each car spilling its load of coal.

As luck would have it, the derailment occurred right outside our hotel door, scattering coal literally on the steps leading to the back door. Our gang spent the rest of the night moving the derailed cars off the track, and shoveling and hauling several hundred tons of coal away in wheel barrels. The next day the railroad sent in trucks to load the coal and haul it back to the yard to be loaded on the coal cars again.

We made several of these trips to other B&O lines, but our main job was maintaining the tracks from Green Spring, in Hampshire County, to Petersburg, in Grant County, a stretch of about 40 to 50 miles of track. Romney was approximately halfway between the two towns, so we kept our speeder in the depot in that town and headed off in one direction or the other each morning, wherever repairs were needed.

I was fortunate to work with three of my brothers-in-law on the maintenance gang. Besides Bill Shoemaker, I also worked with Orville Shoemaker, my sister Lessie's husband, and Willie Curran, who was married to Virginia. Along with two other workers, we would crowd into our speeder each morning and head for trouble spots along the line.

We painted and repaired the depots all along the line, including Green Spring, Romney, Moorefield, and Petersburg. We worked on bridges and rails, which was very hard work, but our worst job was replacing ties.

When we came across a tie that had been damaged or had just rotted out, we pulled the spikes, removed the holding plate, and pulled out the damaged tie. We then inserted the new tie, replaced the plate, and drove the spikes back in. We had a jack that held the rails level, and we would use a square-pointed shovel to throw ballast, which was a filler made mostly of rocks, under the new tie to keep it level.

Shoveling the ballast was the worst part of the job. We hauled the ballast in a compartment in the speeder and carried it to the new tie in a wheel barrel. Hauling, shoveling, and packing the ballast under the tie was backbreaking work that I never really got used to. But the paycheck looked really good at the end of the week, and I honestly didn't have a lot of other options at that time.

10

The war in Europe hung like a dark cloud on the horizon over every part of the world, and our little corner of West Virginia was no different. I heard on the radio news reports about Hitler's exploits, and about all the countries he had taken over. I can't say that I lay awake at night thinking about whether the United States would enter the war, and what that might mean for my future, but it was on my mind from time to time.

But most of the talk at this point was of isolationism. Many people felt that unless our country or its people were actually attacked, then we should not get involved in what for now was a European conflict. Besides, when the first reports about the war in Europe came out, I was only 15 years old and working on the family farm and on Chert Mountain. Country folks have a unique way of focusing on what is directly before them, on the situations and dilemmas that are of immediate concern.

All that changed in 1940. I was still splitting my work time between Chert Mountain and the farm when President Roosevelt signed into law the Selective Training and Service Act on October 16th of that year.

This Act authorized the first peacetime draft for military service in the history of our nation. The original Act stated that all men ages 21 to 36 were required to register for the draft, and that no more than 900,000 men could be in military service at one time. The term of their service was to be twelve months.

The task of keeping track of and registering those eligible for the draft fell into the hands of the local draft boards. There were 6,500 of these boards across the country, with each county containing at least one. The board consisted of three to five unpaid civilians who were appointed by the President on the recommendation of the Governor of each state. The board's duties included tracking young men in their area who were or soon would be eligible for the draft, informing men of their need to register for the draft, and classifying draftees into one of four categories.

The board could also issue deferments to draftees for a variety of reasons. One was the conscientious objector, who refused to serve on the basis of his religion. But other deferments were issued for those with physical problems ranging from false teeth to wearing glasses. Military service was also deferred for married men when the Act was first passed. Lone children who were needed by their parents to work on the farm and those who worked in professions that were deemed necessary to the nation were also eligible for deferments at the Act's inception.

Since these local boards were generally composed of the upper class citizens in the community, rumors swirled that they played favorites with their deferments. Some people, especially the poorer and lesser known people in the county, accused the board of taking care of their friends' children by giving them deferments for any and every reason, while the poor children served regardless of the circumstances. Nothing was ever proved about the board in Romney, and I would be afraid to comment whether these rumors were true or not.

These local boards were under the supervision of the United States Selective Service Agency, which established the order that draftees were to be called by the use of a lottery system. Each man who registered was assigned a number between one and 8,500. The Selective Service Agency then put all the numbers into a drum and drew them out one at a time. The order these were drawn determined the draft order. The first number selected was 158, so all those registered at all the local boards around the country who had been assigned the number 158 were the first draftees in the nation.

Several men in our immediate area were among the first to be drafted. I recall three young men, Frank Tornese, Sammy Bobo, and John Kelley, who were four or more years older than I was, left for Basic Training in 1940. Even though I was only sixteen when the draft started, I began to realize that there was a very real possibility that I would have to serve in the Army or another branch of the Service in the next few years, whether the U.S. entered the War or not.

The Rada Store was a community meeting place where men would gather and sit on the front porch in the evenings and solve all the world's problems. I loved sitting there and listening to these men express their opinions about everything from the War to the Depression to the price of farm machinery.

Right after the draft started and before the U.S. entered the war, some of the boys who had already entered the Service came back on furlough, and they would talk about Basic Training and life in general in the Armed Forces. I recall Sammy Bobo talking about his training to become a gunner on a B-17 bomber. He loved everything about the Service, from the excitement of flying to the military life in general. Sammy was the center of attention, sitting there on the porch in his uniform. Military life was still far away for me, so I thought at the time, but his stories made me wonder about the course my life would follow over the next few years.

But that course became much clearer just a few months later. On December 7, 1941, the Japanese attacked Pearl Harbor, and the United States became a full-time combatant in World War II. Men from all over our area were either enlisting or being drafted, and it became quite apparent that I would be called for service in the near future.

In February of 1942, right after my eighteenth birthday, I received a notice from the draft board in Romney to report for registration. At that time I was not only registered, but I was classified as well. My classification was Class IA, which meant that the board deemed me fit for military service, pending the results of my physical.

Even though my service appeared to be imminent, I can't say that it preyed on my mind. I wasn't told how long it might be before I was called for my physical, and I had a good job that paid a pretty fair wage for the times. So, I continued to go to work each day and carry on with my business. As I said before, simple country folks have a way of focusing on those things right before them and not worrying all that much about the future.

We attended a small community church at that time called Kelly Chapel Church of the Brethren, which was located in Russeldale. During the time between my eighteenth birthday and the date of my Army physical, the pastor and some of the elders of the church talked to me about filing as a conscientious objector to get a deferment from military service. They said that since the Brethren denomination didn't believe in war, they felt sure they could persuade the local draft board to grant the deferment.

Since I wouldn't be serving in the Military, I would be required to serve in some other capacity that benefited the country. A few other men in the area had been granted these deferments, and they were working on farms in southern Virginia. The church authorities said that since I was already familiar with life on a farm, then that type of service to our country would not only be safe, but it would also be enjoyable for an old farm boy like me.

Mother and Daddy also said that, if I didn't want to file as a conscientious objector, they would go to the board and tell them that I was indispensable to the farm, and since growing food was one way to help support the War effort, that I should get a deferment on those grounds. There was a lot of truth in that argument, because the work I was doing and the money I was bringing home from the B&O were of great value to our farm operation, so there really would have been no disgrace in that type of deferment in just about anyone's mind.

But the only mind that mattered to me at that time was my own, and the only person that I had to face was the image I saw in the mirror each morning when I shaved. Many other men had fought in wars and served our nation before me, and I suppose it was a sense of loyalty and patriotism above all else that made me determined to do my part for my country. I told my pastor and the elders at the church that I appreciated their concern for me, but I was going to serve in the Military. I told my parents the same thing, although I'm sure it was hard for them to think about losing a third son.

When the U.S. entered the war, the Selective Service Act was amended to include all men ages 18 to 45. My draft number must have been pretty low, because I wasn't called to take my physical for over a year. It wasn't until shortly after my nineteenth birthday, in February of 1943, that I received a letter from the draft board telling me to report to Romney the third week in July to catch a Greyhound bus to Clarksburg, West Virginia, for my Army physical. I passed the physical with flying colors, and three weeks later I was sworn into the United States Army.

I can't say that I was scared, or that I thought about what could happen to me in a war, but I was a little apprehensive about what lay ahead for me. I had no grand illusions of glory gained through heroism in battle, either. But I was sure of one thing; I owed it to my country to serve in times of trouble, and with Japan, followed a few days later by Germany, the most powerful military nation on Earth at the time, attacking and killing Americans, this certainly was a time of stress and trouble for the United States. I had a job to do for my country, and I was determined to do that job to the best of my ability. So Buck See from Rada, West Virginia, bid the farm and family farewell and headed off to war.

Part Two:
In The Army Now

11

The first step in my indoctrination into the Army was my physical examination. I reported to the draft board in Romney to catch the Greyhound to Clarksburg at 9:00 am on July 21, 1943. The bus, which could haul about fifty passengers, was parked in front of the courthouse, and many of the seats were already taken when I arrived.

All the men aboard the bus were from Hampshire County, but I can't say that I knew many of them. Buzzy Ours, who had gone to college and thus was placed in charge of the bus, was a familiar face, and Junior Bobo, Sammy's little brother, was another that I recognized.

Even though I was a native and lifelong resident of Hampshire County, I didn't get to Romney or other communities all that much to meet other people. My whole life was basically the farm and my work on Leatherman's Orchard and the B&O, so I really didn't know all that many people outside our little community.

The trip to Clarksburg was a real experience. At that time all east-to-west traffic followed U.S. Route

50 because there were no interstates or four-lane highways back then. In fact, Route 50 was what made the town of Romney. Our little burg was a main stopping place for travelers and truckers who were making their way to points west or east. The road went all the way to California, so I was told, although I never actually followed it that far.

The section of Route 50 between Romney and Clarksburg was approximately 100 miles of the most crooked highway on the face of the Earth. It wound up and down steep mountains and through valleys that couldn't have gotten more than a few minutes of sunshine each day. There were hairpin turns up and down those mountains, and I thought we would never get off that snake of a road. But after roughly four hours of creeping up and down those ridges, we arrived in Clarksburg at last.

The room where our physicals were given was some type of huge meeting room in a hotel in Clarksburg. The place resembled a madhouse when I entered, with doctors, nurses, and half-naked men roaming around everywhere. It reminded me of a long human assembly line where we moved along from station to station while the doctors and nurses checked our pulse, blood pressure, sight, hearing, and any other bodily function one could imagine.

Men from all over the state assembled there to be looked at and probed and stuck with needles. I hadn't been to see a doctor hardly at all in my life, and this certainly was the first time I'd ever been given a complete physical examination. I can't say that I cared much for it, but everyone else seemed to be tolerating this invasion of personal privacy, so I went along with it.

After my physical was completed, I dressed and headed into an adjacent room where a man in an Army uniform told us what we could expect next. He first informed us who had passed and who had failed the physical. He had each one of us who passed fill out a paper granting power of attorney to our mother or father or another relative or friend so he or she could conduct our financial business while we were away in the Army. He then said that those who passed would have three weeks to return to our homes and get all our affairs in order before reporting to Basic Training.

In three weeks we were to report to the Induction Center in Fort Hayes, Ohio, to begin our hitch in the Army. By this time it was late in the day, and he told us that the Army had booked rooms for us in the hotel to spend the night. The next morning we boarded the bus once more for the torturous trip back over the mountains to Romney and one last visit at home before Basic Training.

My life went on pretty much as before when I got back home. Mother and Daddy asked me how everything had gone, and my brothers and sisters had a million questions about my physical and what I had seen in Clarksburg. I notified the B&O that I passed my physical and wouldn't be returning to work there. The rest of my time was occupied with helping out around the farm. It was summer, and hay had to be cut; work had to be done in the garden, and crops had to be harvested. I tried to carry on with my life as it had been before my physical. I thought that was the way that I could help my family the most.

I felt no sense of dread or impending doom as my last days of civilian life slipped away. I really didn't think much about it at all. I made up my mind to serve my country, and that's what I was going to do. Had I known what was ahead of me, in terms of training and actual fighting in the War, I likely would have been much more nervous. But the old saying, "Ignorance is bliss," certainly applied to my case. I went about my business and put my military service out of mind as much as possible.

12

On August 12 I boarded another Greyhound in Romney that was headed west to Fort Hayes, Ohio. When I arrived at the Induction Center, the first thing they did was herd us into a room and swear us into the United States Army.

We crossed to an adjacent room and started through another human assembly line, this time to receive our Army clothes. The sergeant in charge told us to take off the clothes we were wearing and roll them into a ball. We labeled our clothes and gave them to another sergeant, who said that they would be mailed to our homes.

We then progressed down a line that contained mountains of Army clothing. We moved from station to station and collected different articles of clothing at each stop. First stop was the duffel bag to store everything. As we moved down the line, the man in charge would hand us a piece of clothing, and the ritual would begin.

The man would shout, " That's a shirt. Hold it up high and look at it. Stuff it in the bag." We held the shirt aloft as though we'd never seen one before and then shoved it into our duffel bag. This procedure was followed for pants and shoes and socks and every other article of clothing we would need until we reached the end of the line. I felt a little silly holding up my laundry and stuffing it in a bag, but I certainly wasn't going to question the Army on my first day there.

After we received our clothes, we walked outside the Induction Center, and I got an idea of just how big Fort Hayes really was. There were rows upon rows of wooden barracks that stretched as far as the eye could see. There had to be several thousand new recruits in various phases of training when we arrived there. Somehow the sergeant guiding us around knew just which one of the barracks was ours, and he took us inside and showed us where to stow our equipment.

The barracks were primitive wooden buildings with bare wood floors. Light bulbs hung from wires attached to the ceiling to provide light. There were twenty iron beds with link springs along each wall, which meant that forty men were housed in each barracks. We threw our mattresses on top of the springs, and those beds were surprisingly comfortable.

At five o'clock, the sergeant roused us all out of our barracks and told us to line up in front of the building. We hadn't been given any instructions on how we were to line up or stand, so we just did the best that we could. After we were called to attention, the bugler sounded retreat, and then we filed through another line where we were handed our bedding supplies.

We retired to our barracks where the sergeant meticulously went over the exact way each bunk was to be made every day. He showed us how to make square corners at the bottom of each bed, and he said that the sheets and blankets had to be so tight that if the inspector flipped a quarter on the bed, the coin would bounce.

The sergeant informed us that there was a bulletin board located outside the front door of our barracks, and that we should check it two or three times a day to see if we had been assigned a duty to perform. He said that there were two different duties, and that it was our responsibility to know if a duty had been assigned to us and to report for that duty on time.

The first was guard duty. We were not given weapons for this duty, except that we did get to carry a Billie club. We weren't looking for intruders or spies, but rather this was a fire patrol. If we spotted or smelled smoke anywhere in our area, we were supposed to report it back to our superiors. The duty lasted twenty-four hours, and we were on duty for two hours at a time and then off for four hours.

The other duty was Kitchen Police, or KP. This was the tough one. We reported for KP at three in the morning and didn't get off until eleven that night. Since we had no alarm clocks, the man on guard duty would come to the barracks and wake us up. He didn't shout or shake the man, but rather he would touch him on the shoulder and tell him softly that it was time to get out of bed.

If he didn't get up, the sergeant in charge of the barracks came in next, and he wasn't quite as nice as the guard had been. He turned the bed over on top of the sleeping man, a most uncomfortable and embarrassing event. I saw this happen on more than one occasion, and I vowed that I would never suffer that embarrassment.

The last thing our sergeant told us was that the lights went out at 10:00 pm. That didn't mean that someone came in and turned off the lights. It meant that the electricity to the lights was cut off at that hour. He said he expected everyone to be in bed and sleeping shortly after ten because reveille blew promptly at five the next morning. Precisely at ten, the lights went out, and thus ended my first day in the Army.

On the way out of the barracks the next morning, I checked the bulletin board, and sure enough, Buck See had KP duty.

Soldiers were arriving at Fort Hayes at all hours of the day and night, so the kitchen and mess hall were never closed. The mess hall had seats for several hundred people at a time, and it was separated into sections. While meals were being served to the soldiers in one section, another section was being prepared for the next wave of hungry men. I suppose that's why soldiers who pulled KP duty worked such long shifts.

All I knew about cooking when I entered the Army was that my mother was very good at it. I had never worked inside at the farm because my services were much more valuable on the outside. When I went to the kitchen, I ate and left the cooking to the women. In the Army there were no women, at least not in the mess hall at Fort Hayes while I was there, so my first day on KP was a real eye-opener.

There were two jobs on KP. The easiest and best was working in the dining area. These men were in charge of clearing dishes and silverware off the tables and putting clean ones in their place. When they set the table, all the silverware and cups and plates had to be perfectly aligned all the way down the entire row of tables. The mess hall had a piece of plywood that the workers laid on the edge of each table that had sections cut out where each utensil and dish was to be placed.

After all the articles had been put in their proper slots, the worker carefully slid the plywood off the table, leaving everything in its perfectly-aligned spot.

I wasn't one of the fortunate ones who worked in the dining hall. When I arrived at the kitchen, the mess sergeant set me in front of a huge metal pot and told me that breakfast would start in a few hours, and the main course would be scrambled eggs. My job was to break the eggs. The sergeant said that two cases of eggs should do the trick. It seemed like an easy enough job until he brought out the eggs. Each case contained forty-four dozens of eggs. I couldn't do the multiplication in my head (that's 1,056 eggs, by the way), but I knew that was far too many eggs for me to break, unless he was talking about breakfast tomorrow morning.

He asked if I could do it, and I told him I had my doubts. He grabbed three eggs in each hand and bashed them together, with the eggs dropping into the pot and the shells remaining in his hands. He said that was the proper way to break eggs in a hurry. He walked away, leaving me to my chore.

I didn't want to scatter eggshells all through the eggs, so I began my task one egg at a time. After several minutes, the mess sergeant returned to scrutinize my work. He looked into the pot and shook his head. He asked me to show him my method, and I grabbed a single egg and cracked it.

He shook his head again, grabbed three more eggs in each hand, and expertly bashed them together. He asked what was so hard about that. I told him that I was afraid to crack six at a time because I would get too many shells in the pot. He smiled and said, "Why would that matter to you? You're not the one eating the eggs."

He walked away disgustedly and mumbled something about seeing if he could get me some help. I continued to break the eggs one at a time, and a few minutes later another man came and helped me finish the job. The mess sergeant then poured the eggs into several huge frying pans that were warming on the stove, and in just a few minutes he had enough scrambled eggs to feed a battalion. I did have some of those eggs, and I couldn't taste the shells at all.

Next the sergeant had me carry in four, fifty-pound sacks of potatoes and plop them down on the floor in front of a chair. He handed me a small metal utensil and told me that the potatoes needed to be peeled so he could fix them for lunch. He said the utensil was a potato peeler, and he asked if I'd ever used one before. I told him that not only had I never used one before, but this was the first potato peeler I'd ever seen in my life.

He gave me that same disgusted look that I'd received when cracking the eggs and jerked the peeler out of my hand. He quickly skimmed the peeler down a potato, and in just seconds he was finished. He placed the peeler back in my hand and told me to get to work.

I worked for at least a half an hour, and I'd barely made a dent in the mountain of potatoes. The sergeant made that peeler sing as he sliced the thin skin off those potatoes, but I just couldn't get the hang of it. I felt like I was improving some when the sergeant returned to check on my progress. He must not have agreed with my assessment of my work, because when he looked in the pot to see how many potatoes I had peeled, I got that disgusted look once more. He walked away again, mumbling that he would try to get me some help. Help arrived a few minutes later, and potatoes were served for lunch that day.

Perhaps sensing that I was inexperienced in the kitchen, the sergeant led me to the sink and told me that I needed to wash up some pots and pans so he could start on supper. I thought there was a mountain of potatoes, but I believe there were even more pots and pans. I stood in front of that sink for hours, and the supply of dirty dishes never stopped. Each time I washed a pan, the sergeant or one of the cooks would replace it with a dirty one.

The sergeant walked in after supper , and I thought he might tell me to head back over to my barracks and get some sleep, since I had done such a good job, like getting out on parole for good behavior. But he had no such idea in mind.

He said the time had come to clean up some around the kitchen, and he handed me a broom, a dustpan, a mop, and a bucket of water. He said the floors had to be swept and scrubbed before he could start on the next day's breakfast, so I'd better get busy. After he turned to walk away, he was the one who got the disgusted look this time.

I swept and mopped and scrubbed and slopped until I thought my back would break or my arms would fall off. I must have been better at cleaning than I was at peeling potatoes, because almost exactly at 11:00 pm, the sergeant, who had also pulled a twenty-hour shift, came into the kitchen and told me to go get some sleep.

Five o'clock rolled around mighty early the next morning, and on the way out of the barracks I thought I'd better check the bulletin board, just in case another duty had been assigned to me. There was my name once more, this time assigned to guard duty.

I reported to my sergeant later that day that I had guard duty the coming night, and he told me that I would be excused from all other commitments that afternoon to get some additional rest in preparation for my 24-hour guard shift. Even though I wasn't overjoyed about serving duty two days in a row, I have to admit the extra sleep I got that afternoon was a welcome relief.

At five o'clock sharp that afternoon I reported to a small wooden shed that they called the guard shack, which would be my home for the next 24 hours. I pulled the first shift, so I circulated around my section of the barracks for two hours and made sure all was secure and that there were no fires burning out of control. After the non-stop action of KP duty the day before, I found guard duty a little mundane.

After my first shift I was allowed to go to the mess hall for supper, which took about half an hour. When I finished eating, I reported back to the shack and spent three and a half boring hours waiting for my next shift. This cycle repeated throughout the night and the next day, and the rest of the time, while a little boring, passed uneventfully.

Except for the down time on guard duty, there was seldom an idle minute during my time at Fort Hayes. We did exercises almost non-stop. We did jumping jacks and deep knee bends and push-ups and sit-ups and running in place until I thought my arms and legs would fall off. These exercises worked practically every muscle in the body. I was young and strong when I entered the Army, but I could feel my endurance mounting with each of these exercise sessions.

We didn't do any drilling while at Fort Hayes, but they did teach us how to line up in an orderly fashion. They first separated us into four squads, each of which contained twelve men. They joined these squads into a 48-man platoon, and then they grouped four platoons into a company of 192 soldiers, plus officers. We followed this configuration whenever we assembled on the parade ground for any reason.

I also was lucky enough to pull KP duty two more times and guard duty once more at Fort Hayes. I was only at the Induction Center for eight days, and I spent five of them in the kitchen and the guard shack. I'm sure it wasn't because I did such a wonderful job or because the mess sergeant requested me. I guess I was just one of the lucky ones.

13

After reveille on August 20, we lined up in our companies and marched to the train station that was located just outside Fort Hayes to embark for our Basic Training site. We weren't told our exact destination, but rumors had been circulating for days that we would train somewhere in California.

We loaded onto what was called a troop train, which was a long train with dozens of cars that were pulled by a coal-fired steam locomotive. Each car carried about 75 or 80 men, and if I had to guess I would say that there were probably 1,000 or more soldiers on the entire train. The cars were bare inside except for wooden tables that had been placed in the center that were bordered by bare wooden benches along both sides. These benches had wooden backs on them and served as our seats and our beds on the four-day voyage aboard that train.

There were a few small windows located at intervals along the sides of the cars, which allowed some light and air to circulate throughout the car. Most of our ventilation came from a big door, in the middle of one side, that slid open. This was the middle of the summer and we were traveling across the arid western part of the United States, so that door was open, day and night, for most of the trip.

I can't say that the trip was enjoyable, sitting for hours on unpadded benches while occasionally nearly suffocating when the wind changed and the acrid coal smoke flooded into our car. We stopped every four hours or so at a train yard, unloaded from the train, and lined up for exercises, just to make sure that we didn't get too bored or too stiff from the ride. When the physical activities ended, we had time to hit the portable outhouses before loading back up and continuing our journey.

The food on the train was surprisingly good. We were served sandwiches at regular intervals, but twice a day, when we stopped for our exercise sessions, we would also be served hot meals from a tent that the cooks set up at the rail yard. The cooks carried the food right on the train and served it family style on the wooden tables. While not gourmet, these meals were hearty and tasty, and we always had plenty to fill us up.

Sleeping was the worst part of the trip. We had some room on the floor, so we would take turns stretching out there, using our duffel bags for pillows. The rest of the time we knapped on the benches, stretching out as best we could or laying our heads on the table. Sleep was never very sound or restful because of the bumping of the train and because the officers kept waking us up every four hours or so to exit the train and get our exercise. But I guess these inconveniences were all part of our training, to get us used to performing under uncomfortable circumstances.

Late in the evening of our fourth day, our journey ended at last near a small town called Riverside, California, which was located about 60 miles east of Los Angeles. When we unloaded from the train I saw this huge air strip with Army planes all around. I could hear the roar of the engines, and I saw a big sign at the main entrance that read March Field. We had no clue at that point what type of training we would be taking, and I thought that perhaps the air corps was in my future, which really appealed to me.

But that was not to be the case. We entered a compound across the railroad tracks from March Field called Camp Hahn, and this was to be our home for the next eight weeks for Basic Training. I noticed that there were several different guns and artillery pieces scattered around the compound, but we still hadn't been told the type of training we would be taking.

The sergeant showed us to our barracks, where we stowed our gear, and then he told us to fall out into formation. After we were lined up, we were assigned to a company and a platoon. We then were herded into a building where our bedding supplies were issued. The sergeant took us back to the barracks and showed us once more the proper technique for stowing our gear and making our beds, so we could be prepared for inspection the next morning.

We then marched over to the mess hall for supper, which I thought was pretty tasty. Many men complained about the food in the Army, but I honestly have to say that I thought the chow was pretty good. The complainers especially disliked a hamburger gravy that was served over toast, which they called SOS, which stood for Same Old Stuff or Something (Crap) on a Shingle. But the food wasn't all that different from what I was used to at home, and I was thankful to have it.

After supper we went back over to the barracks, and our sergeant told us what to expect in the morning. He said reveille was at 5:00 am, and we were to report there neatly dressed and lined up in our proper squads and companies. He told us that the lights would go out at ten that night, and he didn't expect to hear a sound after that.

At ten sharp, darkness fell on our barracks, and my first day of Basic Training came to a close. Rumors flew all around the barracks as to what type of training we would be taking, but the Army hadn't told us anything at that point. As I drifted off to sleep, I thought about how far I'd already traveled, and my training hadn't even begun yet. I told myself that I'd better buckle up, because it looked like I was in for a wild ride.

14

After reveille and breakfast the following morning, we finally found out what our Basic Training would involve. We had been assigned to an anti-aircraft unit, and all those machine guns and artillery pieces that I'd seen the evening before would be part of our training. Every weapon that would be used by our platoon was lined up along the fence around the camp, and our sergeant told us that we would have a choice as to which weapon we would be trained on. He said we could pick three weapons to serve on, and we should prioritize those selections, with our favorite coming first.

We walked down the row of weapons in platoons, and veteran soldiers told us what each weapon was, its use, and the proper method for firing and maintaining it. Two weapons grabbed my attention from the start. One was named a Quad 50, which was a weapon on wheels that could be pulled behind a jeep or other small vehicle. It had a seat in the rear for the gunner and armor plating wrapped around the front for protection. The firepower for the weapon came from four, fifty-caliber machine guns that stuck out the front. As the men explained about this weapon, I could only imagine the awesome power a gun of this magnitude possessed. I could definitely see myself behind those guns, firing non-stop at Japanese airplanes.

But the weapon that really captivated me was the 90mm anti-aircraft gun. Introduced to the Army in 1940, as a solution to aircraft that flew higher and faster, the 90mm was a big cannon that was transported on four bogie wheels that were mounted on a removable axel. A truck or halftrack (a truck with wheels on the front and tank tracks on the rear) pulled the gun in combat.

The 90mm had a barrel that was ten feet long and 90 millimeters (about four inches) in diameter. It fired a shell that weighed 43 pounds and flew at 2,700 feet per second. Its range was approximately 11,000 yards on the ground and 30,000 feet in the air. An accomplished crew could fire anywhere from 15 to 25 rounds per minute. This weapon was a beast and rightfully earned a reputation as a real killer in combat.

Quite an extensive crew was required to move and operate this weapon. The gun commander was a sergeant who was responsible for a gun squad that had a gunner and eight other soldiers. He was also responsible for an ammunition squad that consisted of a chief and two to four ammunition handlers and a chauffeur, who drove and maintained the vehicle that moved the gun.

Once the gun had been moved into firing position, the crew dug a hole twenty feet across and four feet deep for the gun emplacement. The gun was wheeled into that hole and jacked up, and then the bogie wheels were removed. It had four telescoping spider legs that spread around the gun to give it stability when fired, and the crew had to dig additional eight-foot trenches to accommodate each of them. The sand or soil that was removed for the emplacement was shoveled into bags that were piled in front of the gun for disguise and protection. It took quite a while to get everything in place, but once the gun was ready it supplied great firepower.

The 90mm had a platform that ran around the back and sides, and the gunner stood on the right side of this platform. He pulled a lever, and the breech opened and dropped down. The loader would carry a shell up to the back of the gun and lay it in the open breech. The gunner then took his fist and shoved the shell into the barrel. As the shell entered the barrel, the breech closed automatically. The gunner used his fist to push the shell because if he used an open hand he risked losing a finger as the breech closed. The gunner could feel the breech rubbing against the back of his hand as it closed behind the shell. He then stepped away from the gun to clear the recoil and reached up with his left hand and pulled the lever that fired the gun.

The 90mm could be adjusted to fire nearly parallel to the ground to attack enemy troops or vehicles, like tanks. It could be tilted to fire at nearly a 90 degree angle as well. When the angle of fire exceeded 45 degrees, the loader would help the gunner push the shell into the barrel by placing his hand on the back of the gunner's fist to give more strength to the effort.

The guns generally operated in batteries of four, with the same commander in charge of them all. This enabled the battery to concentrate fire on a single aircraft, greatly increasing the likelihood of a hit. Adjustments in the direction of fire could be made manually, with one soldiers controlling the height while the other sighted the horizontal direction. The Army also developed a radar system that allowed the gun to fire at planes that weren't even visible to the naked eye. When the radar was engaged, the 90mm was automatically sighted and fired by that device.

I was totally fascinated by the technology and awesome firepower of the 90mm, and I wanted to be the one pulling the trigger, so my first choice of training was to be a gunner on that weapon. My second choice was to be the gunner on a Quad 50. Once more, I wanted to be the one pulling the trigger and controlling the fire.

The Army developed a range finder to work in conjunction with the 90mm guns, and my third choice of training was to be the man in charge of that apparatus. The range finder consisted of a pipe approximately six feet long and eight inches in diameter, with a telescope on each end. In the middle of the pipe was an opening that resembled a pair of binoculars, where the operator looked to set the distance and range of a target.

When the operator gazed into these binoculars, a set of coordinates appeared in the view finder that told the direction and distance of an enemy aircraft. These coordinates were relayed to the gunner, who adjusted the aim of the gun and fired. I was really fascinated by this device, but it required a special type of eye acuity to operate it, and unfortunately I didn't possess that type of sight.

I'm not sure whether I realized it at the time, but I really wanted to be in a position of authority, or at least be the one in control of each situation I faced. I didn't want to be the one who carried the ammunition; I wanted to be the one who fired it. Leadership qualities that I didn't even know I possessed were starting to come to the surface, even though I was in circumstances that were totally foreign to me.

To my surprise, the Army granted my first choice, and I became the gunner on a 90mm crew. I had no idea at the time how much work and training were involved in this position, but I was glad that I would be working at something that interested and fascinated me.

15

We didn't have an idle moment during Basic Training. Our drill sergeant told us that an idle mind was up to no good, and he did his best to ensure that we had no chance to prove whether that saying was true or not. We studied about the 90mm until I started to consider the weapon a friend, but there was plenty of other, more general, physical training that every soldier, regardless of his assignment, had to go through.

We marched endless hours on the parade ground. At regular intervals we would dress up in our Class A uniforms for a parade before the brass. Inspectors circulated among the marchers, barking out instructions to any that fell out of step. I enjoyed wearing those new, crisp uniforms, and I felt proud of the show of discipline and precision that we started to exhibit.

This show of precision was due mostly to the long hours we spent on close order drill. Any time we had any spare time at all, especially in the evening after supper, we would spend an hour or two working on close order drill, which was precision marching in unison as a squad or company in response to the commands of our instructors. The instructor timed the command so that it arrived when each soldier was taking a step with his left foot. He then took a step with his right before executing the command when the left hit the ground again.

When we first started practicing, we marched off in different directions and sometimes collided with each other. The drill sergeant would stop us all, utter a few choice curse words about our intelligence, and start again. I recall one evening early in my training that I was really having trouble following the commands. I decided that I would trust the man in front of me to lead me in the right direction, so I just started to do everything that he did. This tactic worked for a while, but eventually he became disoriented, and we both marched out on our own in the opposite direction from the rest of the men.

Our drill instructor found out that several men in our company were from West Virginia, so that old stereotype of the dumb mountain man came out. He placed his face about two inches from mine and uttered several epithets about, "You damn, dumb Hillbillies." He inquired whether I knew my right hand from my left and had me demonstrate which was which, just to be sure.

He picked up a rock which weighed at least ten or twelve pounds that he kept handy just for these purposes. He placed the rock in my left hand and told me to keep it there for the rest of the drill, just to make sure that I remembered which was my left hand and foot. It took a while, but I eventually started to enjoy the drilling and the discipline required to perform all the precise commands.

We spent many hours on the firing range target practicing with our M-1 rifles. I had always been a pretty good shot when I hunted squirrels and rabbits and deer back on the farm, so I figured shooting this gun would be a breeze. We had to shoot from several different distances, ranging from 100 to 600 yards, and from different positions, from standing to prone, and we were scored by the percentage of bullets we placed inside the bull's eye, which was bigger for each successive distance.

The M-1 was an incredibly accurate rifle, at least in my hands. Our instructor showed us at the beginning how to set up the sights for the different distances. We kept a booklet at first with all the settings written in it. Once I figured out all the proper settings, all I had to do was hold the rifle steady and squeeze the trigger.

Each rifle had a serial number on it for identification (I still remember mine, 2015356), and it was important to get the right rifle, since its owner had individually sighted each one. Some of the men were haphazard in keeping track of their weapons, which invariably led to problems on the range. I took great care to memorize my serial number and make sure that I had my rifle throughout the training. My diligence paid off, as I earned an expert rating on the M-1 and received a badge to wear on my uniform as proof.

We received instruction in hand-to-hand combat, which was extremely taxing physically. We were taught how to attack with our bayonets. The bayonets were razor-sharp, so we practiced with scabbards on them. I remember one instructor who challenged anyone in our platoon to a bayonet fight. He said that he would keep the scabbard on his bayonet while the recruit could remove his scabbard.

Everyone looked around at each other, wondering if the instructor was serious. After a while one man stepped out and removed the scabbard from his bayonet. He charged the instructor, who deftly deflected the weapon aside and used the butt of his rifle to knock the recruit's weapon from his hands. The instructor's credibility skyrocketed after this episode, and not too many men challenged him after that.

Doing exercises with our rifles was the hardest thing for me. We had to do push-ups, with the rifle beneath our hands. We ran for miles in place, with the rifle angled across our chest. We did deep knee bends where we touched the rifle on the ground in front of us and then sprang up, lifting our weapon over our heads. I hated these exercises, but with each session I could feel my strength and wind improving.

16

Aside from all the drilling and KP and guard duty that we went through, specialized training on the 90mm was extremely hard. We ventured out into the desert for days at a time, practicing setting up and firing the weapon. We started to feel that we were better with a shovel than we were with a rifle, what with all the digging required to set up, disguise, and protect our weapon.

Since Camp Hahn was located in Southern California, most of our practice maneuvers were performed in the desert. Working in sand had its advantages, but it also presented some unique problems. Shoveling out the hole for the gun emplacement was much easier in sand than in regular dirt, and filling up the protective bags with the sand went much smoother.

But transporting the 90mm over that unsure footing was a real nightmare. We tried using a big truck called a Prime Mover that had four wheels on each side in the back and two in the front, all of which provided drive and traction. But at times that vehicle would just sit in the sand and claw away until it buried up to the axels. Then we would not only have to dig a hole for the gun, but we would also have to waste valuable training time digging that truck out of the sand. We finally started to use a halftrack to pull the gun, which made all our lives so much easier.

We fell into a routine each time we went out on bivouac to practice setting up and firing our 90mm. We usually started late in the afternoon, around five o'clock, and we almost always had supper before we started work. The meal was K rations, which were dry or canned foods that were nutritious and could be eaten without any preparations.

The K rations had cheese and crackers and usually some type of canned meat like Vienna sausages or potted meat. The rations included four cigarettes, which I passed along to the soldiers that smoked. For some reason I never fell into the habit of smoking, although it seemed that almost everyone else did. I tried it a few times, but I just didn't enjoy smoking.

The best article in the K rations was the square chunk of chocolate that we had for dessert. I didn't have much chocolate while growing up, and those bars just melted in your mouth. We washed the meal down with water from our canteens, which we refilled from the five-gallon cans that we carried on the halftrack.

After supper, we got down to the serious work of setting up and firing the 90mm. We would pull the gun to a designated spot and begin digging out the hole for the emplacement. It usually took us anywhere from six to eight hours to dig the hole, set the gun, and fill and place the sandbags for protection. We had inspectors coming around constantly to check up on our progress and inspect the operation when we finished. The inspectors promised us that when we finished our work, and it had been inspected, then we could get a few hours of sleep.

But just as we finished filling the last sandbag and putting it in place, the commander would issue a march order, and we would have to begin the entire process once more. We jacked the gun up and placed the bogie wheels beneath it, emptied the sand bags, attached the gun to the halftrack, and pulled out for our next destination. We usually moved and dug in twice a night before the commander would let us get some sleep, mostly in the morning when the weather was the coolest.

The weather was another factor that made our training even tougher. As soon as the sun started rising in the sky, the temperature would start to climb, peaking in the afternoon at well over 100 degrees. But in the evening, just after sunset, we started hunting more clothes to put on. After working in that blazing sun all afternoon, our bodies chilled quite easily once the temperature started to fall.

On one of our excursions it rained for a solid week. Yes, this was the desert, and the locals told us that we were getting more rain in that one week than they usually received the entire year. But the inclement weather didn't halt our training. We dug in through the rain, and shoveling and bagging that wet sand was a real chore. We kept hearing from our officers that training was hard, but that it was mild compared to real combat. If that statement was true, then I began to wonder just what I had gotten myself into with this Army life.

On one of our maneuvers in the desert, we camped near Edwards Air Base, one of the major Army Air Corps (this was before it was called the Air Force) bases. We were used to seeing planes fly in and out all the time at March Field, so the large volume of air traffic wasn't all the unusual to us. Part of our training was to identify planes as they made their final approach for landing at the field. One late afternoon we were working on one of these recognition exercises when we saw a huge plane, by far the biggest we had ever spotted, circling in preparation for landing. As it flew closer, we all speculated as to what type of aircraft it could be.

One of the men in my squad said that he had seen pictures of that plane before, and he thought it was the newest Army bomber, the B-29. It was huge and menacing with the sun glistening off its silver body. The B-29 landed and coasted to a stop, so we all decided that it would be interesting to drive over to the field for a closer look, and maybe even get a tour of this newest war aircraft.

We didn't even get inside the gate. As soon as the plane taxied to a stop, armed guards bearing sawed-off shotguns encircled it until the service men pulled the aircraft into the hangar. But just seeing that bomber gave me new respect for our country's military might.

17

About a week before the end of Basic Training, we finished our field training with the 90mm and headed back to Camp Hahn for some final instructions in preparation for shipping out overseas. We started to pack up all the equipment for shipping to the port in New York, which would be our point of departure. We had trained hard, and I felt like we had bonded into a team that could function well together. The task we trained to perform was at hand, and we were all ready for it.

While our equipment and supplies traveled across the country, each member of our company was granted a fifteen-day furlough to go home and say good-bye to our families and friends. They loaded us into a truck and hauled us to the train station in Barstow early in the morning for our trip home. I traveled to West Virginia via a civilian train, which was much faster than the military model. We didn't have to stop every four hours to get out and exercise, so I pulled into Cumberland two days after I left California.

My sister Hazel picked me up at the station and drove me back to the farm for one last visit before heading to Europe. I loved being back in West Virginia, even if it was only for two weeks. I spent time with my family and friends, and I even went to Rada store in the evenings to help those same old men who had been there when I left for Basic solve all the problems of the world.

Like Sammy Bobo and some of the others before me, I enjoyed being the center of attention when I related stories about what I had done in Basic Training and where I would be going next. And they listened attentively to what I had to say. Just a few short weeks ago I had been a kid who sat and listened to the older men without saying much. But now, I was an equal, a man with an opinion and a story that everyone on the porch wanted to hear. I marveled at the difference three months made in my life.

On the twelfth day of my leave, I woke up early in the morning and knew immediately that something was wrong with me. I tried to lift myself out of bed, but I couldn't move. All the joints in my body (knees, ankles, elbows, wrists, hips, and shoulders) were so stiff and sore that I couldn't force them to work. I finally summoned the strength to roll myself out of bed, but I collapsed onto the floor, unable to stand. I literally slithered out of my room and down the steps to the living room.

Mother heard the commotion and came into the room. She saw me on the floor and asked what was the matter with me. I told her that I couldn't make my joints work, and that I couldn't get up. Alarmed, she asked if I thought she should call the doctor, and I told her I didn't know if he could help me or not, but that she should probably walk to Rada store and call him.

This was the time when doctors still made house calls, and a few hours later Doctor Robert Dailey drove up to our house. He came in and examined me, and he asked what my symptoms were and where my pain was the worst. I explained my situation to him, and he just scratched his head and said that he really had no idea what could be causing my condition. He handed me a bottle of what he called pain pills and told me to take one or two every so often, and that maybe this condition would eventually leave me as suddenly as it had come.

As long as I sat or lay completely still, I had little or no pain, but when I moved any at all, the pain was severe. Not only did Dr. Dailey's pain pills not help any, but as the day wore on I got progressively worse. My return trip to California by train was looming just two days away, and I knew the Army would take no excuse other than my death for being late. But I just didn't know how I would be able to get on the train and endure the ride for two days.

So I hoped. I limited my movements as much as possible over the next day and a half, hoping that my condition would improve. But instead of getting better, I got worse. The pain, which had originally only flared up when I moved, had turned into my constant companion now. I needed help just to stand up, let alone to try to walk. I had no idea whom I should call or contact in the Army, and I truly faced the toughest dilemma of my life to that point.

Seeing no other solution, Hazel drove me to the train station on the scheduled day of my departure and helped me up the steps to the train. I bought a return ticket when I got off the train two weeks before, but this was a civilian train, so the fact that I was in the Military carried no weight. When I walked into the car where I was supposed to have a seat reserved, I was greeted by a mass of humanity. Railroads were the preferred mode of transportation in those days, especially for long-distance trips, because they were cheaper and faster than travel by bus or car.

For some reason the railroad had overbooked this trip, and not one but two other people now occupied the seat I had reserved. I didn't feel right asking somebody else to get up and give me his seat, but I was too miserable to stand for very long. But stand I did. The first stop was in Chicago. I'm not sure how long it took to get there (it was at least eight or ten hours), but it seemed like an eternity to me. The longer we traveled and the longer I stood, the worse my condition got. I was in absolute agony by the time we stopped in Chicago, and I was finally able to sit down.

My situation didn't improve all that much after I got a seat. I still faced another day and a half on the train, and my condition was getting progressively worse. I tried to sleep, but the pain in my joints wouldn't allow sleep to come. I squirmed and fidgeted, trying anything to find a position where I could rest without pain. But all my efforts were in vain, and the happiest moment of my life was the one when the train finally pulled into the station in Barstow, and some men helped me get off.

My battery commander sent a truck down to meet the train because he knew that several of our company who lived on the East Coast would be arriving on that run. Some of the other soldiers helped me up into the truck, and I spent several agonizing minutes bouncing around in the back before we pulled into Camp Irwin at last.

I slept for only a few minutes on an Army cot in a tent that night, and I could only pray that my condition would improve before the morning. My prayers went unanswered, and I felt even worse the next day, no doubt because of the long trip the day before. The pain and swelling made it nearly impossible for me to move at all.

I was finally able to get out of bed and painfully dress myself. I went to my sergeant and explained my situation to him, telling him that I could barely walk at all. One look convinced him that I was telling the truth, and he sent me over to the dispensary in a jeep. They put me in bed at once and gave me some medication for the pain, just as old Doc Dailey had done. Their results were no better than his, and by the next day I was an invalid, unable to sit, stand, walk, or even feed myself. The pain was excruciating and constant. The first sergeant came to visit me, and I told him that somebody had to do something to help me. I couldn't bear the pain, and all I was doing was lying on a cot in this dispensary tent and suffering.

He agreed and called an ambulance to take me to the hospital. They admitted me right away, and their examinations found out no more than the others had. They simply couldn't figure out what was wrong with me. They started giving me pills, but my condition just got worse.

They were experimenting with various medications, desperately trying to find something that would help me. I couldn't even make my hands work well enough to pick up and swallow the medications they had prescribed in mass quantities. A nurse had to watch over me nearly all the time. She fed me and helped me drink, and I was starting to feel like a man who had aged seventy or eighty years in just a few days.

Each day the doctor would visit me, and I would ask him if he had figured out what was wrong with me. He would look puzzled and shake his head and tell me they were working on it but had no solutions as of yet.

After about a week with little or no improvement, the doctor finally said that he thought acute arthritis was at the root of my problems, but he didn't offer much hope that he could cure it. I was taking a whole hand-ful of pills several times a day, but they didn't make me feel much better. The only one that helped was the sleeping pill they gave me in the evening, which al-lowed me to get a few hours of sleep each night.

After I'd been in the hospital over a week, my bat-tery commander came to visit one day, and I overheard him talking with my doctor. He asked the doctor how I was doing, and the doctor told him that I was in pretty bad shape. The commander said that my unit would be shipping out soon, and he wondered if I would be ready to travel with the others. The doctor said there was no way I would be in good enough shape to leave now, and he doubted if I would ever be well enough to serve in the Army. He said the best I could hope for was restricted duty, and more likely I would eventually be released from the Service on a medical discharge.

I felt terrible before I heard this news, but I felt even worse afterward. My country needed me, and I really wanted to answer her call. The Army had taken the time and the money to train me, and now all that training would go to waste if I was on restricted duty or discharged. This news, on top of my medical condition, was almost too much to bear.

On my twenty-seventh day in the hospital, I woke up early in the morning and noticed that most of the pain and stiffness in my joints had subsided. Just as mysteriously as my illness came, it was gone. I got out of bed and walked around the room, astounded that I actually could do those things. The nurse brought me my breakfast, and for the first time in nearly a month I fed myself. As the day wore on, I started to feel better and better. The doctors were amazed. Just as they had been unable to diagnose the problem, they had no idea where the cure had come from.

18

I kept expecting my symptoms to return, but they never did. After a couple of days, the doctor entered my room and gave me a clean bill of health. He said that I was ready to go back to my unit and resume my training. There was just one problem. My unit had shipped out for Europe two weeks before.

The doctor said he would see what he could do, and he started making some calls around the camp. Eventually, I ended up in what was called a Replacement Depot, or as the Army veterans called them, "Repple Depples."

These units were composed of replacement soldiers for those who were killed or wounded in front-line units. Morale in these replacement units tended to be very low because most of the men felt unwanted. They also feared that they would be placed in a unit and situation for which they hadn't been trained, increasing the chance that they would be killed or wounded before they ever found out what they were supposed to do in combat or how to do it.

But there really wasn't much else the Army could do with me. The unit I trained with was already in combat, and no new anti-aircraft units were training at that time. So I went to a designated area in Camp Hahn and waited for three weeks to be assigned elsewhere. I felt fine, as good as I had ever felt in my life, but I didn't have a unit to serve in.

Little did I know at the time just how lucky I was. I talked to some of the men from my anti-aircraft battalion that I ran into later on in the war. They told me that they had been assigned a place in the line near the Ardennes Forest in Belgium. They had been caught in the forefront of the Battle of the Bulge, and the fighting was horrific. Of the sixteen gun emplacements in the battalion, only one had survived. The very gun that I would have been firing was one of the first to be destroyed, with no survivors. The Lord certainly was looking after me, but I couldn't see it at the time.

After three weeks, the sergeant came to our tent one day (I was in the depot with eight other corporals) and told us to pack our gear. We were leaving later that afternoon for Texas. He said that we would be assigned to a new unit once we got there, and after training we would ship out for Europe.

There were perhaps 1,000 other replacements who joined us on the train trip to Camp Swift, which was located in the small town of Bastrop. Camp Swift was a relatively new facility that had just been completed earlier in 1942. Its three thousand buildings had been constructed in just 120 days, and several thousand GI's were there for training when we arrived.

When I got there, I expected to be assigned to a new unit and trained and deployed immediately, but that wasn't the way the Repple Depples worked. Instead, I lay around my barracks for over a month before any decision was made about my future.

And I was treated like a king during that time. The mess hall told us to come by any time during the day, and they would feed us. We had no assigned duties during the day, so we just wandered around the post and looked at all the weapons and machines that others were training on. If word of this treatment ever got out to those fighting in the war, I could see why the veterans disliked the replacements so much.

Eventually the sergeant entered our tent and told us to pick up all our gear and assemble in front of the barracks. He said that it was time that we got involved in the war, and that we would be assigned to units that day. We loaded into the backs of several trucks, and the procession started through the camp.

Every few hundred yards or so, the trucks would stop, and several soldiers would hop out of the back and report to a unit. The truck we were in pulled up to an area that had a big sign that read, "1258th Engineers C Unit," and the sergeant told the rest of us in the truck to jump out. One of the other corporals wondered aloud what the "C" stood for, and I told him I didn't know, but I was pretty sure that we were about to find out.

19

The "C" stood for combat, and we had been assigned to one of the more elite units in the Army. The
Combat Engineers was a specially trained unit that was
capable of performing most engineering duties for its
division. These tasks included demolition, obstacle
emplacement, fortification, and light bridge building.
Normally there were between three and six battalions
in an engineer group, and one or two groups per corps
or Army.

The morale in these units was the exact opposite
of the Replacement Depots. Because these men were
highly trained and skilled, they carried a great deal of
confidence with them into combat. I could tell from the
first time I met the men in my company that they were
special, and they wanted to help me as much as they
could because their lives could be directly affected by
the decisions that I and other replacements made on the
battlefield.

But we ran into trouble from the start. The Combat Engineers had taken most of their specific training
about how to perform all their combat duties at the beginning of their Basic Training, and that had occurred

before we joined the unit. When we got there they were about two weeks from deployment, and they had just started infantry training, which was essential to me and the other replacements because we hadn't received any infantry training at all in our Basic.

Infantry training was a real killer. I really hadn't done much physical activity since I had gotten sick, almost three months before, so I wasn't in the top physical condition that I had been in at the end of Basic Training. We studied troop movements, deployments, and tactics, but the thing we did mostly was march. We routinely marched four or five miles every evening after supper, and we would work on infantry tactics until well into the night and morning. After just a few hours of sleep we were back up and marching again.

I recall one exercise where we had to march four miles carrying all our field equipment, including a backpack, a bedroll, an extra pair of boots, our rifle, and everything else we would be carrying in combat. We had to complete the march in 48 minutes, or we had to do it again until we made the time.

This march was over some of the roughest terrain I had ever seen. I thought Patterson's Creek Mountain was rugged when we drove deer there, but it couldn't hold a candle to the country we covered on that march. There were rocks and steep hills to climb, and some of the ravines we traversed were so steep that we literally had to climb hand-over-hand to get out of them. When we got behind on the time, we had to run to make up the minutes we had lost. The march was real torture, and several of the veteran men didn't make the time, but I did.

After two weeks of almost constant marching (one of our final marches covered 25 miles and nearly left me an invalid the next morning), the commander told us it was time to pack up all our gear in preparation for our trip to Europe. Our first stop would be in England, and the brass promised us new guys that they would catch us up on all the engineering training we missed when we got there.

I can't really recall my thoughts as we prepared to ship out for Europe. I can't say that I was scared, or that I dreaded what lay ahead of me. I really didn't have time to think much at all. We were so busy with our training and with packing up all our gear that all my thoughts had to be kept on the job at hand and on the immediate future. That was the Army way, to keep soldiers so busy with their jobs that they didn't have time to be scared or worried. Yet there were quiet times in the night when I couldn't help but ponder my situation and what would happen to me. At these times I marveled at just how far this old farm boy had traveled to stand on the threshold of World War II.

20

In early October of 1944 we loaded on another troop train at Camp Swift, and around midnight of the following day we arrived at Camp Kilmer, New Jersey. Camp Kilmer was the major East Coast staging area for United States troops shipping out for Europe. Completed just over two years before I arrived, Camp Kilmer consisted of 1,120 buildings, including seven chapels, five movie theaters, a huge hospital, and endless rows of barracks. During the War, over 1.3 million U.S. and Allied soldiers were processed and shipped from Camp Kilmer.

We stowed our gear in our barracks and headed off for a hot meal. The mess hall was enormous and stayed open twenty-four hours a day, because hungry soldiers were arriving and leaving round the clock. After eating, we walked back to the barracks to bed down for the night. I slept soundly after all the excitement of the day.

After reveille and breakfast the next morning, we walked over to a large storage building to receive our combat equipment that we would be taking overseas, including our entrenching tools, backpack, sleeping bag, and winter clothing. After stowing that gear in our barracks, the sergeant marched us over to the barber-shop for one last haircut before shipping out.

We entered a room that had at least twenty-five barber chairs in a long row. Soldiers were being herd-ed through like sheep being sheared. The barbers used clippers without any guard on them, so we had much more skin than hair showing when they finished. I re-member one man who had a well-groomed hairstyle, complete with neatly trimmed sideburns. When he climbed into the chair, the barber asked him if he'd like to keep his sideburns. The soldier told him that would be great. The barber then told him to hold his hands up beside his face, and he caught the whiskers from his sideburns as they fell from the clippers. Everyone laughed, except the man who lost his sideburns.

Later that night most of us had just settled in for what we thought would be a good night's rest when we were roused from our slumber and told to get ready to leave. We dressed quickly, gathered up all of our equipment, and headed for buses that were waiting outside the camp.

It was probably two o'clock in the morning when we finally boarded the buses, and the sergeant briefed us on what we could expect next. He said that we would load onto our ship at night, to prevent any enemy infor-mants from learning what units were shipping out and when. He cautioned us not to speak to any strangers that we may encounter at the port, because even the most casual remark might give the enemy some infor-mation that he could use against us. He was the first, but not the last, person I heard utter the phrase, "Loose lips sink ships."

As we walked up the pier to board our ship, I was amazed at the size of the vessel. The biggest boat I'd ever seen was a rowboat floating down the South Branch of the Potomac, so to say I was impressed by this huge ship would be a great understatement. In peacetime, it had been a British civilian cruise ship that was built to haul 600 passengers. A total of 4,300 soldiers crammed onto the boat for our trans-Atlantic voyage. We walked up the gangplank and headed below to our sleeping quarters. Our home for the next two weeks was one huge room that served as both bedroom and dining room for 1,800 of those soldiers.

We slept on hammocks that were suspended from the ceiling. We pulled them down when we wanted to sleep, and they retracted toward the ceiling when they weren't in use. The ship hauled German prisoners to the U.S. on its trip from Europe, and I guess the maid didn't have time to clean up our bedrooms before we boarded. The hammocks and floor were filthy, and the smell from the Germans , who obviously hadn't bathed in weeks, hung over the whole room.

One side of the room contained rows of tables that were perpendicular to the side of the ship, and each table seated thirty-six soldiers, eighteen on a side, at mealtime. We were assigned seats at the table, and I felt lucky because I drew an end seat that had plenty of space to spread out toward the open room. But I should have known that this luxury came at a price.

When we sat down for our first meal, a sergeant came along and tapped the two men who were sitting on each side at the end of the table on the shoulder. He said that he had a job for us, and that we should follow him. He led us down a steep set of stairs that was more like a ladder. At the bottom of these stairs was the galley where all our meals were prepared.

Nearly every meal we were served on the voyage was some type of soup. Now, I was raised on a farm, and I was definitely not a picky eater. Whatever my mother put in front of me, I ate. But one taste of the soup or stew or whatever they chose to call it that they were serving on the ship told me that I was in for a long, hungry trip. It always had some sort of meat or fish as the basic ingredient, but the main course floated in a broth that was nearly inedible. Grease glared on the top of each bowl, and I could barely force myself to choke down even a few bites of that horrid concoction.

Seeing how the soup was prepared didn't improve my appetite much. When we entered the galley, we encountered huge kettles that were bubbling on a massive stove. The cooks stood over these vats on platforms, stirring the pots endlessly with a long wooden paddle. The smell that rose from those kettles was just short of disgusting. To make the situation even less appetizing, the floor was covered with grease and broth that came almost halfway up my boot when I sloshed through it. The sights, the smell, and the grease made me nauseated even before I tasted the main course.

The sergeant who led us to the galley told us that our job was to be the server for our table. The first thought running through my head was that I hoped the men at my table wouldn't blame me for the way the food tasted. The sergeant handed each of us a container that very much resembled a huge old-time coffee pot, complete with a handle and a spout for pouring, but no lid.

We placed these pots on the platform beside the cook, and he took a giant ladle and dipped up enough soup to fill each pot. I would say that each container held about three or four gallons of soup. We then had to skate across the galley floor through the grease and fat and climb that ladder, which was as slippery as ice from all the residue off the boots of the men who had gone up before, all the while being careful not to slop dinner on the head of the man following us. Climbing that ladder with thirty or forty pounds of sloshing liquid in one hand while hanging on for dear life to the handrail with the other was no small feat.

When we finally got up to the dining area, I walked along the row of men, pouring soup into each man's bowl using a cup that the cooks provided. After I ate as much as my stomach could endure, it was my job to clear all the bowls, plates, and silverware off the table and take them into the kitchen to be washed. We were on the ship for twelve days, and I can honestly say that I never got used to the food. It tasted just as horrible to me the last day as it did the first.

Another thing that made our food situation so unbearable was the meals that the British cooks ate on the trip. While we soldiers had that awful soup for almost every meal, the cooks feasted on steak and chicken and fish. Many were the times that I wanted to throw that soup container at the cooks when I saw them sitting down to a juicy steak for supper.

As if to rub salt in our wounds, the cooks would often gather up the scraps of meat or fish that they were too full to eat and make them into sandwiches. They would then walk among the soldiers and sell these sandwiches for as much as five dollars apiece. They offered one to me at that price at the beginning of the voyage, and I told them I'd rather starve than pay that much for the food that we were supposed to be getting in the first place. After two weeks of that soup, I was closer to starvation than I cared to be, but I still refused to pay those outrageous prices for a sandwich.

Seasickness was a real problem for many of us. A vast majority of the soldiers had never sailed on a ship in their lives, so that constant up-and-down motion as we plowed through the waves got to many of them just after we left the harbor. Men lined the railing of our deck at all hours of the day and night, hurling up that awful soup from the previous meal. I felt fine the first two days of the trip, just long enough to fool myself into thinking that maybe I would be lucky and not get seasick. Boy was I wrong! The third day I woke up nauseated, and the feeling just got worse as the day wore on. Breakfast brought on my first trip to the rail, and I was a regular visitor for the next week.

I just felt terrible all the time. But I still had to report to meals and make that harrowing trip down and back up that ladder to serve the few soldiers who actually had an appetite and could stomach that horrible soup. The smell of the galley and the soup, and the greasy slop on the floor, certainly didn't help my queasy stomach much. I hadn't been sick hardly at all while I was growing up, so this constant nausea made my life miserable. By the time we finally left the ship in England, I had lost several pounds, most of it over the rail into the cold Atlantic Ocean.

21

Our ship reached England late in the afternoon of the twelfth day of our trip, but instead of unloading right away, we dropped anchor and waited for darkness to fall, I suppose so as to not expose to the enemy what units were arriving at that time. At about nine or ten that night, the ship moved close to the shore, dropped a ramp, and we waded ashore to Europe. I don't think I've ever been so happy to arrive somewhere in my life. I could have kissed the ground when we walked off the ship, but I don't think the others in my platoon would have appreciated that very much.

We boarded Army trucks for the three-mile trip to our training facility, which was located in a small village called Newton Abbot, some sixty miles from London. When we arrived at our quarters, they weren't traditional Army barracks, but rather they were houses that belonged to English citizens who had been evacuated to other parts of the country. These homes were far from fancy, but they were comfortable, and we would look back on those quarters as some of the best we had during the War.

When we arrived in Newton Abbot, we assembled and Captain Hahn, our company commander, told us that each soldier would be issued one serving of K rations. He told us to put them in our backpacks, and that was all. Since it was so late when we got into town, the cooks didn't have time to set up the kitchen and feed us, so some in our company ate the K rations before going to bed. The rest, including me, went to bed hungry.

The next morning, before going off for training, we had coffee and a cold sandwich for breakfast, so by the time we marched six miles to the training site we were all starving. Every man who hadn't eaten the K rations the night before did so at that time, including all the officers. When we returned to quarters that evening, we assembled once more, and Captain Hahn told us that, since the kitchen was now up and running, he wanted each of us to return the K rations we had been issued the night before, since we hadn't been given orders to eat them.

Our platoon leader circulated among his men, asking if anyone had K rations to turn in. He was greeted with lots of sheepish grins but no rations. Needless to say, Captain Hahn was less than pleased when he heard the report. We assembled once more, and he announced that we had failed to follow orders, even though none had been given. As a punishment for this lack of discipline, we would embark on a twenty-four mile march to give us time to think about this lapse in discipline. He designated Lieutenant Horton, a short, raspy-voiced man who must have been the commander's whipping boy, as the leader of the march. After dinner, we were to return to the barracks, pick up all our gear, and reassemble for the exercise.

Now the men, especially Lieutenant Horton, were the ones less than pleased. Our march began, and every three miles or so we would stop for a short break. During one of these breaks, probably at the six-mile point, I happened to be close enough to Lieutenant Horton to hear him griping. He said that if he wasn't certain that S.O.B. of a company commander was sitting in his jeep at exactly the twelve-mile mark, we would turn around right there and tell the brass that we had completed the whole march. Sure enough, when we reached the turn-around point, there sat Captain Hahn in his jeep with a broad smile on his face. I'm not sure what he was trying to prove with that type of discipline, but the result was a whole company full of men who despised and mistrusted him.

Our training facility was located six miles from Newton Abbot, and since trucks suddenly seemed to be in short supply, we marched to the facility each morning. Our training site was a large field that covered several hundred acres and had every type of assignment that we would face once we went into combat.

I'm not sure whether the veterans in my platoon were used to working with live explosives or not, but I have to admit that I was a little nervous when our training first started. I had never even lit a firecracker before, so the idea of blowing up a bridge or building was totally foreign to me.

We started our training with land mines. These were mostly the pressure-triggered mines that were designed to explode when someone stepped on them. Our assignment was to learn how to lay these mines following a specific pattern, and how to detect and retrieve mines that had already been deployed.

We practiced these exercises in conjunction with another platoon. We would lay a minefield in one area, while the other platoon would also lay a field in its sector. We then traded positions, picking up the mines that the others had deployed. They told us where the perimeter of the field was located, but that was all. It was up to us to figure out what pattern (mines were always spread out in a pattern) they had followed and then pick up the mines without blowing ourselves up.

Using a mine detector that very much resembled a modern-day metal detector, but with a much larger and more sensitive receptor on the end, a two-man crew would start on the edge and mark a path to the center of the minefield with tracer tape. Once we determined the pattern the mines had been laid in, the rest of us would move to the center, very carefully following the path that the crew had cleared, and pick up the mines, fanning out from the center in four directions.

To retrieve the mines we first had to determine the pattern in which they had been laid. There were only so many patterns to follow, and once a few mines were detected we could figure out the pattern. Each of us would then pick a row, and we would disarm all the mines in that row.

To disarm a mine, we would slide our bayonet under and around the mine to expose the firing mechanism. All these were pressure mines that had a firing device similar to a hand grenade. When the mine was armed a pin was pulled, allowing the mine to compress when stepped on and explode. To disarm the mine, we had to carefully replace that pin, which held the mine in place and kept it from exploding when we picked it up.

I was more than a little nervous at the beginning, especially that first time I stepped into a live field and followed the path that others had cleared for me. I was literally putting my life in someone else's hands. But I rapidly learned to trust my fellow soldiers, just as they learned to trust me. Like any other job or skill, practice led to improved performance and confidence, and after a month of training I felt confident that I could perform these tasks in combat.

I saw more than a few tragedies even before I entered combat. One day early in our training, we were waiting on the mine detector crew to finish marking a path into a field when our beloved company commander drove up in his jeep. He hopped out and headed toward our location. He saw the two men with the detector several hundred feet away, and for some reason he thought that they weren't doing their job.

He called over our platoon leader, Lieutenant Goodson, and ordered him to get down to those men and stop the foolishness before someone got killed. Lieutenant Goodson, who had been with this platoon since its inception and knew full well the dangers involved, apparently wasn't paying attention as he walked through the field. I saw him wander to the edge of the tracer tape and then step no more than a few inches outside the tape. There was an explosion, and he rose four or five feet off the ground.

Two or three of us raced into the field, gathered him up, and carried him to safety. Once we got him out of the field, we laid him down, and I saw that nearly all the meat on his legs, from his feet to his hips, had been blown away, leaving just the bones exposed. He was alive, but mercifully, he was unconscious. There was no ambulance handy, so we loaded him on an old air compressor truck that had toolboxes on each side and hauled him to the hospital. We visited him in the hospital a couple of times before we shipped out, and he said that he would be going home in the near future, but I never heard if the doctors were able to save his legs.

Some of us may not have had enough respect for the power of even a small block of TNT before the accident, but we gained a whole new respect for it afterward. We were required, for obvious safety reasons, to wear our helmets and keep our faces in the dirt when digging around mines, but I'd often seen men out in the middle of a field with no helmet before the accident. A land mine employed a one-quarter pound block of TNT, which was about six inches long, three inches wide, and one inch thick. It was hard to believe that something that small could carry much of a kick. But after the lieutenant was blown four feet off the ground, we all realized how dangerous our work was, and we maintained a sense of safety thereafter.

Even though the accident was clearly Lieutenant Goodson's fault, I still felt that it wouldn't have happened had not Captain Hahn butted into our business. I know it was his job to see that the men were working efficiently and safely, but this time he simply drove up and made a rash decision that had cost us a great leader. I served under many superiors while in the Army, but I can honestly say that I never had a better commanding officer than Lieutenant Goodson.

However, I can't say the same for Captain Hahn. Even before the K rations incident, a strong sense of animosity had begun to mount against him. I mentioned that my platoon had completed nearly all its specific training before I got to Texas, but we did one engineering job before our infantry training started.

Military bridge construction had not kept up with

technological advances in other facets of warfare. New pontoon bridges, which had only recently replaced Civil War technology, were almost obsolete before they were employed. These new bridges could withstand a payload of up to twenty tons, but the newest tanks the Allies were building weighed nearly twice that much.

A British engineer, Sir Donald Bailey of Britain's Royal Engineers, invented a new bridge in 1940 that carried his name. The Bailey bridge was a metal span that came in eight- to ten-foot sections that snapped together as they extended over a river or other stream. These bridges were portable and easy to construct, and many generals felt their development and implementation were one of the turning points in the War in Europe.

Our job in Texas was to construct a Bailey bridge over the Columbia River. The Columbia was a big stream, probably a hundred feet wide and ten to fifteen feet deep in the middle. It carried quite a strong current that could be very dangerous. We finished the bridge, and a tradition among the Combat Engineers was for the commanding officer to walk to the middle of the bridge upon completion, and the men would throw a bucket of water on him to christen the bridge for motor and foot traffic.

I wasn't very familiar with the other men or Captain Hahn at the time, but I had started to sense that the men weren't very happy with their commander. They left little doubt about their feelings when Captain Hahn strutted out onto that Bailey bridge. Two soldiers slipped up behind him and tossed him off the side of the bridge into the cold, swift, deep water. They even admitted later that they hoped he couldn't swim, and if he drowned, the brass would think the incident had been a harmless prank that had gone horribly wrong. To their dismay, the captain managed to swim to safety, and he acted as if the whole thing was a joke, but the hard feelings that came from that incident never left our company.

I ran afoul of Captain Hahn the first day after I arrived at Camp Swift. He called me into his office and reamed me out for not having a proper haircut. I explained to him that I had been in the hospital for over a month and just didn't have the time to get a haircut before reporting to Camp Swift. He gave me until that afternoon to get a haircut and told me to report back by a certain time so he could make sure that I had followed his order. That was an example of his type of discipline. The men in his company were on the verge of mutiny, and he was worried about one man's haircut. Sometimes he simply couldn't see the big picture.

It was funny, but I recognized my need for a haircut even before Captain Hahn did. Earlier that day, before the captain called me in, I asked a good buddy of mine, Eugene Waldrop, if he would loan me enough money for a haircut because in all the confusion of my being in and out of the hospital, my pay hadn't caught up with me yet. Before he could loan me the money and I could see a barber, Captain Hahn called me on the carpet about it.

Eugene turned out to be one of my best friends in the Army. We served together throughout our stint in Europe, and when we parted at the end of the War, he gave me his address and told me that if I was ever in Georgia to be sure to look him up. Nearly fifty years after we last saw each other, I made a trip to Fort Benning, Georgia, to see my grandson at a change-of-command ceremony when he returned from duty in Somalia. On my way back to West Virginia, I decided that I would stop in Lagrange, Eugene's hometown, and look him up.

I had long since lost his address, and likely it wouldn't have been the same after all those years anyway, so I went to the phone book and started calling everyone with the last name Waldrop. On my fourth try, a lady answered the phone and told me that Eugene was her husband. I told her who I was, and she gave me her address and invited me over for a visit.

When I got to her home, she sadly told me that Eugene caught pneumonia and died about a year before. We had a long talk about Eugene's life, and she showed me many pictures from the War, one of which was identical to one that I pulled from my wallet and showed to her. We ate supper and reminisced about our families and the lives we'd built after the War. I was really sorry that I missed seeing Eugene, but I had a very good feeling about my friend after that long conversation with his wife. It was almost like I had been with him through all those years. Eugene was the only one of my friends from the Army that I ever tried to visit.

But Captain Hahn got what he deserved in the end. An officer from the Inspector General's Office showed up at our camp two weeks before we went into combat. He interviewed every man in our company, and he asked each of us how our training had gone and if we had a problem with any of the officers in our outfit.

Nearly every man mentioned the unfair discipline that Captain Hahn had employed, and some even went so far as to imply that the captain might not last too long in combat. Nobody came right out and said it, but the inspector understood the underlying message. If the Germans didn't get the captain, then one of his own men might squeeze off an accidental round that would do the trick. A week before we deployed into combat, Captain Hahn was transferred out, and a new commander from Headquarters Company took his place.

22

After we finished our training on land mines, we moved on to other explosives. We worked with primer cord, which was a rope-like explosive about as big around as my middle finger that came rolled in a coil. We measured out as much as we needed, wrapped it around whatever we wanted to blow up, added a fuse, and lit it. We wrapped primer cord around trees as big as two feet in diameter, and when the cord went off it sawed that tree off as neatly as if a chainsaw had done the job.

We practiced using Composition C, which was a putty-like compound that would stick to whatever we wanted to blow up. Composition C was especially good for wrecking railroad rails. We put the explosive on top of and around each side of a rail and added a fuse, and when the Composition C went off the rail became a useless pile of twisted metal.

We were drilled endlessly on safety precautions. Our company commander told us over and over again that we wouldn't do anybody any good if we were dead. We'd been specifically trained to do a job, and chances are that job wouldn't get done if we'd been killed.

One aspect that he harped on continually was the length of the fuse we used to detonate the various explosives. We had a manual that showed how long each fuse should be for each charge, but he told us that a good rule of thumb was to make the fuse long enough that we could turn around and walk away from the explosive, not run. If we ran, there was a chance that we would stumble over something and fall, thereby putting us in danger when the charge went off. If we walked, we could be sure that we had made the fuse long enough to do the job.

I have to tell you that the hair stood up on the back of my neck every time I lit a fuse and strolled away from it. Even though I had followed the rules and set a fuse long enough to allow me to walk to safety, there was still that hint of doubt until I had walked out of harm's way.

Life in England wasn't all work and no play. We trained five and a half days a week, but Saturday nights and all day Sunday were pretty much our own time. I guess the Army figured that we needed some relaxation time before heading off to combat.

The USO sponsored dances every Saturday night in a joint called Ford Hall. As one might expect, the alcohol flowed, and occasionally fights would break out over which company or soldier was the best or toughest. But at the end of the evening, we generally left as friends, and the fun we had there helped to break the tension that accompanied our constant training and the threat of our first taste of war.

Now, English girls seemed to be quite fond of us American soldiers, and they would just happen to be passing by our quarters at precisely the time we were all leaving for the dance every Saturday evening. I recall one night when I had made a date with one of the English girls, but when I arrived at the place where we were to meet to go to the dance, she wasn't there. Another girl that I had dated in the past walked by, and I struck up a conversation with her to pass the time until my date arrived.

A few minutes later, my date walked up and immediately started yelling at the other girl. She said that I was her date, and that this other woman better just move along. The other girl fired back that if I was such an important person in her life, then why was she the one standing there talking to me. I took a step back and waited for things to develop.

I didn't have to wait very long, because my original date took a swing at the other girl and landed a solid punch to the side of her head. The other girl staggered backward but then recovered and started throwing punches of her own. Much scratching and clawing and hair pulling and cursing ensued, and I stood amazed that two women could actually be fighting over me. I made up my mind that the winner of this scrap would be the lucky girl who accompanied me to the dance that night, providing she could still walk after the fight. My original date emerged victorious, and she really didn't look that bad, considering all the rolling around and scuffling she had been through.

A week or so after that episode, I met an English girl at the Saturday night dance, and we eventually became quite an item. Her name was Eunice Hammercott, and she lived in the little town of Newton Abbot where we were stationed during our training. She would walk from her home to meet me at the house where I was staying, and we would walk together to the dance. She was a wonderful girl, and as time wore on we became rather fond of each other. Even after I shipped out for the European mainland, she wrote me faithfully to tell me about her life and all the things that were going on in England. I started to have thoughts that perhaps we would get married some day.

Eunice's father was an engineer in some big company in England, and her family was pretty wealthy. After the War she invited me to come back to England for an extended vacation before I shipped out for home. She said that her father would foot the bill for all the expenses. She also said that, if it was alright with me, her father would pay for her to fly to America after I went home, just to meet my family and get to know them better. She said that she could fly into New York, and I could meet her there after I was discharged from the Service.

I knew full well what she had in mind. She wanted to get to the U.S. so we could get married. I really liked her, but for some reason I just didn't feel that she was the woman that I wanted to marry. She was nice and very attractive, but I just couldn't envision being married to her. Maybe it was the difference in our families and customs that gave me those doubts. Whatever the reason, I wrote her back and told her thanks, but I would be going back home without her. She was devastated when she got the news. She wrote a couple more times, but I never saw her again.

Our advanced training stretched on for over a month, and with each passing day I became more accustomed to the routines of the job and more confident in my ability to perform competently and safely. Apparently this confidence showed to my commanding officer as well. I arrived in England as a corporal, but I would make sergeant before we actually went into combat.

About two weeks before we were ready to deploy into combat, my commanding officer approached me while I was standing in line for a movie. He pulled me aside and told me that he had been watching my progress in the training exercises and felt that I was ready to take on a leadership role in the company. I was already an assistant squad leader, but he asked if I would be interested in stepping up to become a squad leader, a duty that was accompanied by a promotion to sergeant.

He said that he wasn't pleased with the sloppy performance of our current squad leader, and he felt that once we entered combat, someone with more self-discipline and pride would be needed to lead the squad into battle. He was sure that I was the person for that role. All this praise caught me completely off guard because I honestly didn't know that the lieutenant viewed me in such terms, especially since I was a relative newcomer to the company. He said that if I accepted the job the announcement would be on the bulletin board the next day, stating that I was now a sergeant and a squad leader.

I asked if I could give him my answer in the morning, and he said yes, but no later. I spent a restless night considering the promotion. Up to that point I had only been responsible for my job and my own safety. If I became a squad leader, then I would have twelve other men to look after and worry about. Everything would have to be done with the health and safety of those men in mind. This was not a responsibility that I considered lightly. The next morning I told him that I would be honored to become a squad leader, and I was immediately promoted and put in charge of the fourth squad.

And so, at last, my training was over. After nearly a year and a half, the journey toward World War II that I began in July of 1943 with my Army physical was about to begin in earnest. I was healthy, well trained, and in good spirits as I headed for the mainland to tackle the best that Hitler's Germany had to offer.

I embarked on my journey without fear, because now I had other men's lives in my hands, so I hadn't the luxury of being scared. Their survival depended on the decisions that I would make once we went into combat. I was still quite apprehensive about what combat would be like and how I would handle pressure situations under fire, but I had confidence that the training I received and the discipline that had been drilled into my brain from my first day in the Army would carry me through any tight spots. My country needed me, and I was about to answer the call.

Part Three:
War Really Is Hell

23

After dark on December 24, 1944, Christmas Eve, we boarded a small British ship at a port in England for the eighty-mile voyage across the English Channel to France. The air was cold and damp as we loaded in the darkness, and by the time we landed at Cherbourg there was probably three or four inches of snow on the ground, and the snow was still falling steadily through the bitterly cold air.

We gathered our gear and assembled on the outskirts of town, and our company commander told us that we had a little walk ahead of us before we could find a place to sleep. We marched five or six miles away from the port and up a range of hills to a plateau that had a large field that was filled with short, scrubby evergreen trees. The captain told us that this field would be our home for the night.

By this time (it was probably three or four in the morning), the snow had accumulated to perhaps six or seven inches, and it seemed the temperature had plunged even more. Since we knew we would be moving on in the morning, we didn't bother to set up our one-man tents for protection from the elements. I just found a small clearing in the trees, tore off some branches and placed them in a pile on the snow, threw down my poncho, and unrolled my bedroll on top of it.

Our bedrolls were issued to us at Camp Swift, and they were one of the best and most useful pieces of equipment in the entire Army. I could throw that bedroll down anywhere, in the mud or rain or snow or freezing temperatures, and I would sleep warm and dry through the night.

After about an hour of sleep, our sergeant circulated through the field of sleeping men and told us to rise and shine and gather up all our belongings because we were moving out. He said that the cooks had hot coffee and donuts for breakfast. We walked to the mess tent and bolted down as many donuts and cups of coffee as we could in the minimum time allotted and assembled for our march.

We retraced our steps back down off the hills that we climbed the night before and marched to a train station outside town. The train was made up of what were called "forty-and-eight cars," which were designed to haul forty men or eight horses. They had a big door that pulled shut on the side, and they were empty except for a large canvas bag that was suspended from a tripod in the middle of the car. This apparatus was called a Lyster Bag, and it contained thirty-six gallons of clean drinking water that we could use to fill our canteens from the six spigots that surrounded the bottom of the bag.

By the time forty soldiers, along with all their equipment, crowded into one of those boxcars, there wasn't a lot of extra room, especially with that big bag of sloshing water in the middle. The Lyster bag swung back and forth to the rhythm of the train, and each time it swung some of the water slopped over the top onto the floor. We had everything that the Army had issued to us, including our duffel bags with all our clothes, our bedrolls, and our rifles, along with us, and soon water had seeped into everything.

Conditions were miserable on that train. There was barely room enough to stand up and move around in the boxcar, and there were no bathroom facilities. If we had to urinate, we made our way through the pile of soldiers to the door and let it fly. If we had to defecate, we just had to wait until the train stopped, which happened twice a day. At these train yards where we stopped, the cooks had set up tents, and they served us hot meals, which were a welcome relief from the K rations we ate all the rest of the time on the train.

We spent four terrible days, including Christmas Day, on that train before we finally reached our combat destination. This was the second consecutive Christmas I had spent away from home, and I stopped to reflect on just how far I had already come, and yet my journey was just beginning.

24

The troop train pulled into the station for its final stop in a small village somewhere in Luxembourg. As had been the case when I departed from the ship that carried me to Europe, I felt like kissing the ground when I got off that train, but I knew the others in my platoon, especially the men in my squad, wouldn't look too kindly on that maneuver.

Luxembourg was one of the countries that Germany had conquered early in the war, mostly without shedding blood, but you couldn't tell that by the time we arrived there in late 1944. Most of the towns were nothing more than isolated piles of rubble, and the farms had been stripped of both crops and livestock to feed the Nazi armies.

When we got off the train, we were less than half a mile from the front-line fighting, and we got our first taste of the sights and sounds of war. It was late at night when we arrived at the town, and we marched to a small building in the middle of the tiny village to get a little sleep.

Our company commander came in as we were spreading out our bedrolls, and he told us what we could expect the next day. He said that the Germans were making a push to break through at this town, and that it was our job to stop that push. He told us that another division had been sent in a circling movement to get behind the German forces and cut them off, but it would take some time to complete that maneuver. It was up to us to hold the Germans in their place until the other division was ready to strike.

We then bedded down on the floor in our bedrolls, and I remember hearing machine gun and mortar fire off in the distance. I told the members of my squad to get some rest because the time had come for us to get into the fray.

As I lay there listening to the not-so-distant sounds of war, the reality of my situation began to sink in. I was going to be in battle the next day, and all my thoughts were centered on my men and how they would react to their first taste of combat. None of us had fired a shot in anger yet, and I just hoped that I would have what it took to lead men into battle and perform the many tasks that I had been trained for over the past eighteen months. I spent a restless night mulling these issues over in my head.

A good portion of my training with the Combat Engineers had been infantry training, and that instruction came in very handy during my first few weeks in combat. We arrived in Luxembourg at our appointed destination and time, but our engineering equipment hadn't been quite so punctual. In our training we were told that we were infantry first whenever needed, and engineers second. That philosophy proved true for the first two months of my service in the wartime Army.

We were in a holding position on a steep ridge that overlooked the town and the valley leading up to it.

Each afternoon at around dusk, my squad moved onto that ridge to keep track of enemy movements during the night. Our orders were not to engage the enemy and not to get into a firefight if they confronted us. If the Germans attacked, we were to defend ourselves and fall back to the safety and support of the other troops in the town.

We stood our watch in foxholes that had been dug by the previous company that had occupied that position. These foxholes were about five feet deep and three to four feet wide. It had been snowing ever since we arrived in Luxembourg, and perhaps a foot of snow had accumulated on the ground. In the daytime, when the temperature rose above freezing, that snow would start to melt.

Since our position was spread out along the side of a pretty steep ridge, the water from that melting snow ran down the ridge and accumulated in the bottoms of our foxholes along the way. The first night we deployed along the ridge, I picked out a foxhole that was centrally located among the others in my squad so I could keep an eye on them and relay orders as quickly as possible. I shared my foxhole with another man who served as a runner to communicate information back to the company commander.

When we got to our foxhole just before dark, we found about six inches of water in the bottom. We baled the water out with our steel helmets and found some brush to pile in the bottom of the hole. We chopped up some small branches with our pointed shovel and threw them on top of the brush to keep us up away from the water that was sure to seep back in during the night. We left the middle of the hole open so we could bale the water out as it accumulated on the bottom.

We stood our guard through the night and then returned to town just before daylight the following morning. All our movements were made under the cover of darkness to conceal them from the enemy. The cooks had set up a mess tent on the outskirts of town, and they served us one hot meal a day, usually around noon. The rest of the time we lived on K Rations.

After the first day my squad, which was attached to Headquarters Company, moved our sleeping quarters to a small abandoned farmhouse on the outskirts of town. The civilians who owned the house left their home with just the clothes on their backs, leaving all their household belongings behind to be gobbled up by whichever army controlled the town at a particular time. We found beautiful China plates and dishes, and I loved the grandfather clocks in the house. The first thing I did when we moved in was wind the clock so I could hear it chime every fifteen minutes. I would have loved to bring one of those clocks home with me, but it wouldn't fit in my duffel bag.

The first night out on watch we were all understandably nervous, and we were convinced that each sound we heard was a German slipping up for a sneak attack. We first came under fire about four hours into our initial watch when the Germans opened up with a mortar barrage that lasted several minutes that seemed like several hours. Most of the rounds landed well behind us, but we could hear the shrapnel whizzing through the air above our heads after each shell exploded.

I have to tell you that we were all pretty nervous while those mortar rounds rained down around us. The worst part was the whistling sound each shell made as it descended toward our position, which was followed by several agonizing seconds of silence before the round exploded. I kept my head down and made myself as small as possible on the bottom of that hole until the shelling stopped.

But I didn't scream, and I didn't run, so I guess I passed my first test under fire pretty well. Fortunately, I was the only one who knew just how scared I really was. That's the thing about fear in combat. It's a very private and personal emotion, and those who can keep those feelings in check and go about doing their jobs while still recognizing the dangers involved are the ones who make the best soldiers.

I mentioned that I shared my foxhole with a runner, and I soon found out why the Army used this arrangement. We had crank-up phones that we used to communicate with headquarters during our watch, but every time the Germans unleashed a mortar attack, the phone lines, which lay exposed on the ground, were shredded by the flying shrapnel, thus necessitating the use of the runner to maintain contact with headquarters. New lines were run each day, but nearly every night they were destroyed again by the enemy. The first assignment of my runner each night was to get to headquarters to tell them that we would be communicating by runner because the phone lines were out again.

Occasionally the communications men would venture out at night to patch the wire or run new cable, but they were nervous about doing their job out in the open in an area where another mortar attack could be just moments away. Most of the time when they did establish communications again, another mortar barrage would soon follow, and the line would be ruined again, wasting all their efforts.

I have to say that it was comforting to know that at least we had a lifeline back to headquarters when the phones were operational. We felt might lonely out on that hillside when the phone lines went dead, especially the first few nights we were stationed there.

Tension hung over us like a thick fog as we peered out into the darkness and listened for the slightest noise that was out of the ordinary. We had several false alarms, but we were there for nearly two weeks and never fired a round at the enemy. We heard later that the Germans found out about the division that was moving in behind them, and they evacuated their position during the night.

25

We were attached to the First Cavalry Division while we were stationed in Luxembourg. The Combat Engineers was an elite outfit, but I have to admit that the First Cavalry was superior to just about any unit that I encountered during the War. With their roots dating back to the beginning of the Civil War, this division was composed of mostly veteran soldiers who knew their job and took it seriously. Although no longer mounted on horses, the First Cavalry still carried a confidence and a swagger like no other I encountered in Europe.

Members of that unit would often slip out at night to infiltrate German lines to capture prisoners that could help us detect enemy strength and movements. We would see them in pairs or groups of five or six as they crept past our positions, headed for the enemy encampment. They were masters at avoiding direct confrontation with the Germans. They preferred to single out an individual sentry or guard and capture him without alerting the main force of the enemy. When the First Cavalry went after a prisoner, they seldom came back empty handed.

One night shortly after we moved into the front lines, one of the corporals in my squad crawled up to my foxhole and said that he had heard something unusual in front of his position. This marked the first time that anyone from my squad had made such a report. He said that he just knew that a whole platoon of Germans was waiting to ambush him.

I told him to calm down and return to his post. I said that if anyone came within earshot of his foxhole that he should challenge him with the password to find out if he was friend or foe. If the intruder couldn't supply the correct answer (we were given a new password and response each evening before we went out on watch), then he knew what he had to do to defend our position.

The corporal returned to his foxhole, and shortly thereafter he heard rustling in the brush in front of him. He challenged the noise with the password, and a man replied that he was from the First Cavalry out on a mission to capture prisoners. He said that he left that evening before the new password was given, and that he didn't know the right response. He also related that he had stepped on a land mine and was bleeding to death.

This was the moment of truth for this corporal. He had been cautioned before he entered the line that the Germans were skilled in all types of intrigue, and that they would make up any story on the spur of the moment to get the edge on their opponents. This corporal had a very big decision to make, and his life, as well as the lives of many of his companions, hung in the balance.

Luckily, the intruder helped him to make that decision. He said that he didn't know tonight's password, but he did know the password and the response from the night before, and that he would be glad to give the corporal both. After a brief pause, the corporal told the mystery man to give him that information, and when he gave the correct response the corporal told him to advance.

A member of the First Cavalry then crawled up to the corporal's foxhole. He had the lower part of his right leg missing because he had stepped on a land mine. Blood was squirting from the wound, and the man was so weak that he could barely speak above a whisper.

The corporal yelled for help, and I responded. Fortunately, this was one of the few nights that our field telephone was operational, and I called back to headquarters to tell them we had an injured soldier. The medics came up to our position and took the man back to the field hospital. I learned later that he made it back to England and was expected to survive.

Even though we were green to combat, we all learned a valuable lesson that night. The members of the First Cavalry who went on those covert missions were experienced volunteers who had seen just about every type of situation and danger that one could face in war. They knew full well that if they were shot or injured they were on their own. The mission wouldn't stop to treat a wounded soldier.

We discovered from that man that experience and knowledge are extremely important in combat, but those elements don't always carry you through. Sometimes on-the-spot judgment and pure luck are greater factors in survival. As I watched the medics put that wounded warrior in the ambulance, I wondered what fate, or luck, had in store for me the rest of that night and in the future.

26

While we were busy standing watch over the Germans in Luxembourg, Hitler was busy launching his final offensive further to the north in Belgium. Early on the morning of December 16, 1944, the German dictator unleashed a savage attack through the Ardennes Forest that caught the U.S. troops, who had been stationed in this remote part of the front for rest and refitting, completely by surprise. Over 200,000 soldiers and nearly 1,000 tanks spearheaded the offensive that would eventually be called The Battle of the Bulge.

Thinking back to his glory days of 1940, Hitler sought to drive to the English Channel and split the Allied forces. He planned to capture and employ fuel and ammunition dumps that he encountered along the way, and he felt that the Allies, who he surmised were weary of the physical, financial, and emotional strains of war, would be inclined to sue for peace, thus saving face, and averting possible destruction, for Germany.

But instead of panicking after this unexpected offensive, General Eisenhower saw this not as a crisis but as an opportunity. The Germans were on the offensive and exposed, and the time was ripe to strike at them and inflict as much damage as possible on their thin ranks. The Bulge looked scary on paper, but in reality this was the chance the Allies had been hoping for.

But first that initial surge had to be checked. Huge gains by the Germans in the first few days caused grave concerns as the Nazi motorized units closed in on the Meuse River. But as the days wore on the U.S. troops began to stiffen, slowing the Germans at vital bridges and crossroads. Desperation stands by American forces at St. Vith and especially at Bastogne became front-page news around the world.

I mentioned earlier that Combat Engineer groups, which consisted of three to six battalions, were assigned to the various Armies that were serving in the European Theater. At the time when The Battle of the Bulge first started, my battalion was assigned to the Third Army, which was under the command of General George S. Patton. The Third Army was engaged with the Germans in Luxembourg, but at a staff meeting held in the first few days of fighting in The Bulge, General Eisenhower asked what troops could be employed to bring relief to the embattled forces trapped in St. Vith and Bastogne.

Without blinking an eye, General Patton said that his Third Army could be in position to attack the enemy in Belgium within two days. It was a brash statement from one of the toughest and most brilliant commanders the Americans had, but it was a promise that General Patton intended to keep.

Although we weren't in the first wave of General Patton's Third Army that sped north toward Bastogne, we moved into the battle when the Germans broke through at several strategic points and threatened to strike at the flanks of the U.S. forces. Trucks arrived in our little village a few days later, and we loaded up for the harried trip north to Belgium.

It was cold in Luxembourg, but Belgium was another case altogether. As the steady stream of tanks and trucks slid along the icy country roads, the temperature plunged and the snow piled up. It was cold when we used to travel by wagon to Patterson's Creek in January and February to cut ice chunks, but I have never experienced cold like I felt in Belgium. My hands and feet were never warm as we plowed through the constant ice and snow.

But even worse than the cold and snow was the destruction that we witnessed along the way. We passed through St. Vith, which by the time we got there had changed hands between the Allies and the Germans five times. There literally were not two bricks on top of each other. The entire town was nothing more than scattered, useless rubble. A few civilians straggled through the village and waved at the trucks and tanks, and I couldn't help but think about the useless death and destruction that the War had inflicted not only on the soldiers from both sides but also on the millions of civilians who were lucky enough to escape with their lives, but little else.

Our engineer equipment still hadn't caught up with us yet, so my squad, along with all the other Combat Engineer units, joined the front lines of the fighting. We walked behind or beside, or occasionally rode on, tanks as they blasted their way across the Belgian countryside. It was a great comfort to have those mechanized monsters beside us to offer protection from small arms fire and firepower to attack the enemy at long range.

Our battalion traveled in a specific pattern as we wound our way across Belgium. Tanks, supported by infantry, would fan out in waves that were designed to entrap or surround the enemy. Often, the Germans would sense the trap that we were setting for them, and they would retreat before the jaws could be snapped shut. I fought for nearly a month on the front lines in Belgium, and we seldom faced a direct confrontation with the enemy.

But that didn't mean that the fighting didn't take its toll on all of us. Tension gripped our ranks nearly all the time. We hadn't faced much resistance from the Germans up to that point, but the possibility of an ambush or a major battle lurked over every hill. Nearly all of us, especially the members of my squad, were green recruits who had never faced the enemy in mass numbers. That may have been to our advantage because we didn't understand all the dangers involved and the brutality of armed conflict. And the crippling cold and ever-present snow added to our misery.

We passed through several small towns on our way across Belgium, and the Germans had a penchant for retreating ahead of our columns but leaving small elements behind to fight surprise, delaying actions to try to slow down our advance. Many were the times that we thought we had cleared all resistance from a town only to be attacked from the rear by enemy soldiers who had been overlooked as we swept through.

To remedy this situation, General Patton chose two courses of action. The first was an all-volunteer unit that came to be known as the "Snow Ghosts." This unit was nearly invisible, dressed in their all-white uniforms while traveling over the snow-covered landscape. These "Snow Ghosts" actually traveled ahead of the infantry and entered towns secretly to try to obtain information about the enemy's strength and deployment. They were instructed to never get into a firefight with the enemy if detected, but rather to retreat immediately to the safety of the columns that were following them. The information they were able to garner proved invaluable to the infantry that was plotting strategy for an attack.

The General also selected one or two platoons to remain behind after the main column had passed through a town to roust out any stragglers that the Germans left behind to surprise us. I'm not sure whether it was by accident or by design, but many of the Engineer units were tabbed for this duty.

For the most part, these mop-up duties were pretty mundane, but occasionally we would stumble onto an ambush that the Germans had left for us. In one small town that looked like almost all the others we passed through, my squad was assigned to sweep one sector, and as we were creeping down a side street we heard someone bark the order, "Halt!"

We knew that no other American forces were in the area, so we figured that the Germans were employing an old tactic where they would confront American soldiers with a surprise order to try to get them to give away the password for that night. Luckily, nobody in my squad replied with the password, but I have to admit that the hair on the back of my neck was on end for the rest of that patrol.

Some other squads weren't always so lucky. That same night a man from another squad blundered onto a pocket of Germans holed up in a basement room of a bombed-out building. Rather than waiting for help, the soldier burst into the room, right into a grenade that the Germans threw in his direction. The grenade exploded just as he entered the room, and he never had a chance. He was still alive when his comrades got him to the aid station, but I'm not sure he made it through the night. His lack of judgment had likely cost him his life.

Another tactic that we employed was stationing listening posts at strategic locations on the outskirts of town to try to detect enemy movements in preparation for a surprise attack. These listening posts were scattered out over a four or five mile radius around the perimeter of a town, and since they were temporary stations, no telephone communication was established.

To check up on these listening posts and to receive any information they gathered, one squad leader was designated to visit all the posts every two hours. I was the man tabbed for this duty on more than one occasion. I had a jeep that I kept at a central location, and every two hours I made the lonely trip around the circuit to see what was happening. I carried a Thompson sub-machine gun across my lap for protection, but I couldn't help but think that the Germans could see and hear me in that jeep long before I could detect their presence. But like so many other tight spots and duties that I saw during the War, this one also passed without incident.

27

After about a month of fighting on the front lines, our engineer equipment found us at last, and we began to perform the tasks for which we had been trained. We were assigned to the Third Army, but we were attached to whatever division needed us at a particular time. I can recall being attached to General Patton's 94th, 97th, and 99th Divisions at various times throughout the War.

By mid-February of 1944, the Bulge had been driven back, with the loss of some 150,000 soldiers between the two armies, and General Patton began to hammer away at the German homeland. We moved into the Saar Valley, a vital area to the Germans both strategically and economically. The broad valley was considered the gateway to the heartland of Germany, and one of the richest coalfields in Europe supported a thriving steel industry that was essential to the German war effort.

In the Saar Valley our Combat Engineers outfit finally got down to the business for which we had been trained. We followed right behind the infantry units as they moved from town to town, eliminating German opposition along the way. Once the infantry took a town, it was our job to come in and clear all booby traps that had been left behind and blow up the pillboxes and other fortifications the Nazis had abandoned. We blew them up so, if the Germans took back control of the town, they wouldn't have these fortifications to fight from again.

My squad was issued a 2½-ton truck to haul our supplies. That truck was basically an ammunition dump on wheels. We needed explosives to blow up the pillboxes, but the Army had trouble filling our demands, so we improvised. When we had any spare time at all, my squad could be found scouring the countryside for shells and bombs that had failed to detonate (we called them "duds"). We would take anything from a German 88mm artillery shell to a 500-pound bomb. Our truck was equipped with a type of winch system that enabled us to load and unload the heavier ordinance.

We developed a real knack for finding those duds. If there was a bridge nearby, we could usually count on finding an unexploded bomb in that area. Sections with heavy fortifications, like railroad yards and road crossings, were also prime spots for the picking. We would pile the explosives in a pillbox or other fortification, add a small amount of TNT as a primer, light the fuse, and wait for the fireworks to start.

We had been trained how to disarm duds, but I was still quite nervous the first few times we removed the fuse from a shell or bomb and loaded it on the truck. My mind told me that, unless the shell fell off the truck, or we had a wreck, the ordinance wouldn't explode, but there was still a nagging doubt in the back of my mind as to whether my training had been complete.

But like any other skill, once we practiced it a few times we were much more sure of our abilities, although we never became careless or complacent in our handling of these high explosives. We had seen too many buildings and pillboxes completely destroyed by a shell or bomb to ever take their power for granted.

The German pillboxes were marvels of modern construction. It was evident that the Germans contemplated and prepared for war far in advance of the declaration of hostilities. These pillboxes were often buried so that only the slits for firing their weapons were exposed. The walls were thick, reinforced concrete, some of which were sturdy enough to withstand everything except a direct bomb hit. The doors, which were generally located on one side, were solid steel and virtually indestructible.

The infantry trying to take those pillboxes had to crawl up under withering machine gun fire and throw explosives into the pillbox to kill everyone inside. This was the German homeland, so those same soldiers who had been so eager to retreat in France and Belgium and Luxembourg were now determined to fight to the death to protect their land and their people. I had great admiration for the soldiers who repeatedly risked their lives to capture and eliminate these strong points.

I recall one pillbox that illustrated the German ingenuity and workmanship. We were outside a small town somewhere in the Saar Valley, and we could tell that extra care had been taken when constructing one particular pillbox, but we had no idea just how strong it was. We took several shells and piled them atop our normal charge of about one hundred pounds of TNT that we used as a primer charge. We lit the fuse and walked out of the pillbox, and when that charge went off, we expected to see the walls collapse, but to our surprise the door, which was six inches of solid steel, flew open, but the pillbox remained intact.

Knowing we couldn't bypass such a strong fortification, we went to a nearby bridge and found a 500-pound bomb that had failed to detonate. We removed the fuse, loaded it on our truck, and headed back for another try. We placed the bomb next to another 100-pound primer charge, lit the fuse, and walked a safe distance away. When that charge went off, the steel door flew about ten feet in the air, and the walls of the pillbox split open like one of those eggs I cracked back at Fort Hayes. We found out just how serious the Germans were about defending their homeland when we measured those walls and found them to be six feet thick with steel reinforced concrete.

28

The next obstacle General Patton and his Third Army faced was the Siegfried Line. The Siegfried Line was first constructed before World War I on the border between France and Germany. Static fortifications were all the protective rage in warfare at that time, and the Siegfried Line was built facing the French Maginot Line, with both countries feeling secure behind these protective walls.

Much of the Siegfried Line was destroyed during World War I, but Hitler could still see the usefulness of a protective barrier near his border, so he reconstructed the Line bigger and stronger. Even though mechanized warfare had somewhat rendered static defenses obsolete, you couldn't tell that to the men of Third Army who had to get through the Siegfried Line on the road to Berlin.

The Line was an intricate web of obstacles designed to make an American soldier's life miserable. The first line of defense was a series of mine fields that were laid strategically on both sides of the Line. Next came what were termed "Dragon's Teeth," which were concrete obstacles that came to a point on top and were about four feet high and three feet wide at the bottom. The base was sunk three to four feet into the dirt, making them almost impossible to push out of the ground.

The Teeth were placed just close enough together that a tank or other vehicle couldn't squeeze between them. There were two rows of these Teeth, and the second row was staggered with the first, setting up a maze that motorized vehicles had to navigate. A tank with relatively new tracks could crawl its way atop the Teeth, but once it went forward, it would likely wedge between the two rows and be rendered a hindrance to any tanks that followed.

If a tank managed to get over or through the Dragon's Teeth, it next encountered a moat-like ditch that was slightly wider than a tank was long and fifteen to twenty feet deep. Without the aid of some type of bridge, the tank would plunge into that ditch, never to be seen again. Plus, there were machine gun nests and other gun emplacements strategically located along the Line that could bring to bear tremendous firepower directed toward the tanks and the infantry that followed them.

The scope of these fortifications was incredible. Standing on a hill next to the Line and gazing in both directions, I was amazed to see the Dragon's Teeth stretching as far as the eye could see. Millions of hours of labor went into the construction of these obstacles, but all that work was rendered useless once our armored divisions breached the Line and rolled relentlessly through the heart of Germany.

The Combat Engineers were the ones assigned the task of punching a hole in the Siegfried Line so the armor and infantry could roll through. Working during the day was virtual suicide, so we started our job after dark. The Germans didn't have enough men or equipment to lay minefields the entire length of the line, so our first assignment was to pick an area that wasn't mined.

We then crawled up to the Dragon's Teeth and placed TNT charges at the base of enough of the Teeth to allow tanks and trucks and other equipment passage. We blew the Teeth, and then bulldozers pushed dirt into the moat until a solid base was created that could handle the weight of the tanks and trucks. We felt a great sense of pride when the tanks and other vehicles rolled through the hole we created in one of the Germans' last lines of defense.

29

Even though we were no longer on the front lines, there was still great danger involved in the lives of the Combat Engineers. We were continually thrust into positions where the enemy could get a clean shot at us, but we didn't have either the weapons or the opportunities to fire back. That was never more evident than when we were called upon to transport troops across rivers.

Shortly after we broke through the Siegfried Line, we settled in a small, nameless German village that was on the banks of the Saar River. Across the river was a plain about 500 yards wide that led to another small town. The Germans were encamped in that village. We watched them move around during the day, and I'm sure they kept an eye on us as well. Neither side seemed overly enthusiastic about messing with the other.

In fact, about the only time that any fireworks erupted was when the First Cavalry pulled into town. They had this 57mm gun on two wheels that they towed around behind a jeep, and every day or two they would pull maybe ten or twelve of those guns into the town where we were staying and line them up along the riverbank at the edge of town. They would fire them off in unison at the Germans across the river and then pull away.

When we heard those 57mm guns fire, we headed for cover because we knew that in just a matter of minutes the Germans would answer those shots with an 88mm artillery barrage. The First Cavalry, which had stirred up the trouble and then pulled out, was miles away when the 88's started raining on us, and we had to pay for their fun. As I scrambled for cover, I just couldn't see why the First Cavalry didn't let a sleeping dog lie.

One of the scariest moments I had during the entire War came during one of those 88 barrages. This one wasn't the First Cavalry's fault. The Germans opened up unexpectedly, and several members of my squad and I got caught out in the open. We didn't have time to get into the basement of a building, our normal shelter, so we dived into a low spot beside an old stone church.

The Germans were lobbing shells over the church into an open field that was on the same side as our hiding place, and as each round exploded I could hear the shrapnel whizzing through the air and splattering against the stones over our heads. I'm not sure how long the bombardment lasted, but I had plenty of time to ponder my mortality before the shelling finally stopped.

During that same attack, one of the men in my squad found out the power of an 88 shell. He was standing guard near an inside doorway at company headquarters, and one of the first shells in the barrage entered the house where he was standing and detonated right above that doorway. The concussion from the blast blew him completely across a large conference room and slammed him against the far wall. He was dazed and confused for several hours, but all his parts were in the correct place when the medics checked him out. He was a very lucky man indeed.

It was a pretty common practice when the two forces were in that close proximity for one or the other to sneak across the river at night, slip into the other town, and capture a prisoner who would hopefully supply information about the enemy's strength and intentions. Sometimes one side would send a patrol just to nose around and pick up any information that they could about the enemy. These were covert operations that, when executed properly, were accomplished without firing a shot. I mentioned before that the First Cavalry was extremely adept at these maneuvers.

Some officers had huge egos, and they were constantly trying to prove to themselves and the other officers that the men under their command were the toughest and bravest in the entire Army. These officers were not true leaders, because they certainly wouldn't do the dangerous things that they asked their men to do. They were egomaniacs who puffed themselves up by sacrificing the brave men under their command.

The commander of the battalion to which we were attached, or perhaps someone further up the chain of command, must have been that kind of leader. Either the battalion commander or his superior ordered that a patrol be formed out of volunteers, and their assignment would be to sneak across the river and creep close enough to the enemy to gather information about the Germans' strength.

They were ordered not to get in a firefight with the enemy, but if they were fired upon they would return fire while retreating back to the safety of our side of the river. The crazy part was that they were to carry out this assignment during the day, not at night. I was no military genius, but it sure sounded like a suicide mission to me. To expect men to cross 500 yards of open field in daylight without being detected and drawing fire seemed like madness.

The only advantage the men would have was a maze of trenches the Germans had dug in the field for their own protection. Perhaps if our men could get in those trenches without being detected, they would have a slight chance of getting close enough to spy on the Germans. But that chance was very slight in the daylight.

I wasn't at the meeting where the commander asked for volunteers to participate in the mission, but I'd bet dollars to donuts that nobody was thrilled by his proposal. I know I wasn't that thrilled when I discovered that my assignment was hauling the patrol across the river in a pontoon boat in broad daylight.

Ten enlisted men and one officer were selected for the mission, and I had to make two trips because my boat wasn't big enough to haul them all at once. When the first group piled into my boat just before dusk (I couldn't help but think that we could have waited another hour or so until it got dark), I felt like a real sitting duck while we paddled for the far shore, which was probably 200 yards or so away. I held my breath as I waited for the mortar or artillery barrage to begin at any moment. The Germans surely had to see us coming.

But no shells came, and when I finally got both loads of men across the river, we met at a spot where the bank rose perhaps fifteen or twenty feet to the level of the open field beyond. The commander of the patrol drove a stake in the ground at that point and tied a piece of fine wire, which was on a spool, to the top of the stake. He told me to unwind the wire as I paddled back across the river and tie it to another stake on the far side. He figured that it would be dark before they were ready to return, and when his patrol got to the river he would pull on the wire to let me know that they were ready to come back.

I got back in the boat and paddled for the far shore as those brave men climbed the bank and headed straight toward the enemy. When I got back to the friendly side, I scaled the bank and watched the patrol edge its way through the trenches toward the first house on the outskirts of the town. When they got within 100 yards of that house, the Germans opened up with everything they had on those poor souls.

Mortars exploded all around them, and withering machine gun fire pinned them to the ground. They returned fire as best they could and started to retreat. As soon as I saw the Germans attack, I jumped into my boat and headed for the opposite shore.

Bullets whizzed over my head as I paddled across the current as quickly as my arms could pull. I felt even more like a sitting duck than before, but I had no choice but to carry out my duty and help out those desperate men.

The only thing that saved me was the bank on the far side. Any bullets that were low enough to hit me slammed into the bank, and the shots that cleared the bank flew over my head. But I didn't have time to think about my good fortune at the time. Every one of those bullets seemed to have my name on it, and I expected at any time to be wounded or killed.

When I arrived on the other side, I spent several uneasy minutes before the first men vaulted over the bank and scrambled up to me. They told me that one of their men had been wounded, and they had carried him through a trench further down stream. I pulled the boat to the place where the man was hiding and loaded him and half the passengers in with me. The man was bleeding profusely from a head wound, and his comrades had bandaged him and applied sulfa powder as best they could.

Bullets continued to whiz over my head as I dumped my first load and started on the return trip. The tracers were the scariest. These were illuminated bullets that told the direction of fire so gunners could adjust their aim. I didn't mind so much the bullets I couldn't see, but those tracers told me just how close all the ones I couldn't see were coming to my head.

I picked up my last load and started back for friendly shores. As soon as we touched down, our side opened up with machine guns and artillery. It was quite a show as the two sides exchanged blows across the river. Before long, the German guns fell silent, and a few minutes later ours went still as well. Believe me, that was a fireworks show that I won't ever forget.

Despite the asinine decision to send out the patrol in the first place, all the men miraculously returned alive. The wounded soldier had been hit just below the right ear with a machine gun bullet. The bullet entered the skin and followed the contour of the back of his head, exiting just below his left ear. The ambulance was waiting to take him to the hospital as soon as my boat touched the shore, and the last I heard was that he was going to recover.

30

There was no doubt that both sides kept a pretty strict watch on the enemy. We were aware of the situation, so any moves we made close to the river were executed after dark. Each squad was assigned a house close to the riverbank, and each evening just after dark we would head to our house to stand watch on the river that night.

One evening we must have been just a little early, and as we walked between two houses, we heard the German 88's open up. The Germans obviously had that space zeroed in with their artillery. The gap was only twenty-five or thirty yards wide, but the shells started landing so fast that we only had time to hit the dirt where we stood instead of scrambling for cover.

Livestock, especially cows, roamed all around the town, and we often used them for fresh milk and sometimes even fresh steaks. Their revenge was the manure they scattered throughout the town. When the first shell exploded, one of the men in my squad dived head first to the ground, and as luck would have it, right in the middle of a fresh cow patty. He spit and he cussed and he swore that not one cow would be alive the next day, but his dilemma was a welcome relief from the tensions of war, even though he failed to see the humor in the situation.

The house we stayed in was a two-story dwelling, and members of my squad were on watch both upstairs and down throughout the night. Half the squad stood watch while the other half got some sleep. After four hours, they switched. I was asleep one night when one of the men who were watching from a second-story window nudged me awake and told me that he was hearing strange noises from an adjacent room upstairs. He said that he was just sure that the Germans had somehow sneaked across the river and were preparing an ambush.

He led me up the steps to the door of the room, and he repeated that Germans had to be in the room. I told him he was crazy, but I offered to go inside and check it out. I put my ear to the door, and sure enough, I could hear something moving around in there. Even though I knew the chances were pretty slim that any Germans could have slipped into the house without our knowledge, I have to admit that I was a little hesitant to turn the doorknob and walk into that room.

I decided that my best strategy was to catch them by surprise, so I drew back the butt of my rifle and slammed it into the door. The door flew open, and I burst into the room, my rifle at the ready. I certainly surprised the intruders, because a whole row of chickens, which had been roosting on the headboard of the bed, flopped away in all directions. At least I think they were surprised; it was very dark in the room, and you can't always tell what a chicken is thinking from the look on its face.

All those little German villages looked pretty much alike, and I never could keep all the names straight. We stayed in so many as we moved across Germany that they all started to run together. We would move in right after the infantry, often staying in the same houses that the infantry had occupied hours or the day before. The German civilians were in such a hurry to move out that they took only the clothes on their backs with them when they hit the road. We found all kinds of treasures in those homes, from fine glasses and dishes to rare collectibles and clocks.

We spent one night in a two-story house that was similar to many of the others we stayed in. Just after daybreak, I was awakened by a crashing sound coming from the second floor. I crept up the steps and discovered a member of my squad, a Jewish boy from New York, sitting before an open window. He had found a stash of quite expensive dishes that the owners of the house had hidden in a closet. He was mumbling to himself, and every few seconds he would grab one of those dishes and hurl it out the window. The dish would land on the slate roof of the house next door and explode into a million pieces.

Each time a dish broke, he would laugh hysterically. My first thought was that he had cracked under the strain of war. I spoke to him, but he didn't even acknowledge my presence. I walked closer and repeated his name, and this time he jumped as if coming out of a trance and looked up at me. I asked him if he was OK, and he said he was fine. I then asked him what in the world he was doing.

He said that he was just repaying the German people for starting this war and dragging him thousands of miles from his home. He was risking his life every day, and the way he figured it was that it was all their fault. I told him to carry on, and turned to leave the room. As I pulled the door shut, I heard him mumble, throw another dish that exploded on the roof, and laugh as if he'd gone crazy. Everyone, at one time or another, had to blow off a little steam, and I figured there were much more dangerous and foolish things he could be doing than breaking a few dishes.

I mentioned before that we often moved into a house just minutes after the infantry moved out, and the first thing we had been trained to do was go through the place to search for booby traps and other explosives. The infantry moved out of one house in particular one night around 3:00 am, and we literally entered the door as they were exiting. We were dog-tired (we hadn't slept in over forty-eight hours), and we figured that if the house was safe enough for the infantry it would certainly be safe enough for us. We plopped down wherever we could find an open space and were fast asleep just a few seconds later.

The next morning we started to look around, and we discovered just how lucky we had been. No house that we stayed in before compared to the surprises the Germans left for us in that place. Every door had a trip wire attached to it so when the door was opened a homemade bomb would explode. There were several old desks and chests in the house, and every drawer and compartment in every one of them was booby-trapped. We spent nearly an entire day finding and dis-arming those explosives.

The men noticed that the drawers were slightly open in one of the old desks in the house. They carefully checked it out and discovered that nearly every inch was booby-trapped. They gently carried the desk outside, moved a safe distance away, and fired a round from an M-1 through it. When the explosives went up, we couldn't find a piece of wood big enough to make a matchstick. Had that desk gone off inside the house, there would have been nothing left of it.

One of the men from my squad walked into the cellar and discovered a strange-looking pile of hay in one corner. As he moved closer, he could hear a ticking sound. He carefully moved some of the hay and discovered that the ticking was coming from a timer that was attached to a 500-pound bomb. He looked at the timer and saw that it was set for three days, but he had no clue when that three-day timing period had started. As far as he knew, those three days could expire at any second.

He flew up the stairs and told me what was going on, and we evacuated to a safe distance immediately. The company commander felt that we couldn't leave with that bomb there to possibly kill some of our own men or some civilians, and we didn't have the time to hang around, keeping everyone out of the area, until it exploded when the time expired. The only solution he could think of was that somebody had to go back into the cellar and disarm the bomb, since all the Combat Engineers had been trained in disarming explosives.

We were told in our training back in England that every explosive had to be set by someone, and the bomb was designed so the person setting it would be able to get away. There had to be some type of timing or trigger device that set the explosive off, and disarming it was as simple as finding and removing that trigger. We had trained on explosives with timers, but I don't think anyone in my squad had disarmed one as of yet.

This was much too dangerous an assignment to order someone to do it without first asking for a volunteer. The man from my squad who had discovered the bomb said that he felt like it was his job, so he volunteered. I pulled him aside and asked him if he was sure that he wanted to do this, and if he was sure he knew what to do. He assured me on both counts. He was in a foreign land thousands of miles from his home, and yet, out of concern for his fellow man, he stepped up to do the job. I admired the courage he showed, while at the same time I agonized over his welfare.

The soldier walked into the house and disappeared. Everyone on the outside was eerily silent after he entered the house as though our silence would somehow help him do his job. He seemed to be gone forever, although in reality it was only about fifteen minutes. The door flew open, and the man walked proudly out of the house with the biggest grin I'd ever seen, holding the timing device high in the air. His courage exemplified the fighting spirit of the American soldier.

The Germans were infamous for their use of explosive surprises. It got to the point that we were almost paranoid when we entered a town or building, which I suppose was part of the reason for setting those traps. If they could kill just a few men with these tactics, it would make all the other Allied soldiers more cautious and deliberate in their movements.

Allied soldiers, and Americans in particular, had a strange attraction and fascination for a German 9mm pistol called a Luger. It was a powerful weapon that was the standard-issue sidearm of the German Army. Its magazine held eight bullets, and the weapon was known for its balance and accuracy. Plus, it had unique lines that attracted American soldiers like a moth to a flame.

The Germans knew how much Americans prized these pistols, so they used that desire against us. The Germans would often leave a Luger on a dead soldier, knowing that an American soldier would likely come by and spot it. They would attach a small explosive that they hid under the dead man's body to a trip wire so when the pistol was removed, the explosive would detonate. I saw one man from another squad killed by this tactic.

31

My squad was an odd mixture of personalities and cultures from all across the United States. In that sense, I guess it was a good representation of the United States Army in general, with many different types of people rallying to a common cause in defense of their way of life.

I mentioned about the night we arrived in Luxembourg, when we first heard the sounds of war. We had just settled down for a few minutes of sleep, and each man was alone with his thoughts about the War. I'm sure most of the men wondered what they were doing there and what would happen to them the next morning when actual combat became a reality. But most of the men, if they were suffering, did it in silence.

Not so with one of the men in my company. Up to this point the man had caused little or no problems. He was the typical soldier going about his business and doing his job as best he could. But perhaps the pressure got to him on this night.

We'd only bedded down a few minutes when a soldier named Mooring, who hailed from South Carolina, sprang to his feet and began cursing at the man in the bedroll beside him. He said that no S.O.B. was going to crowd him out of his spot, and that if he did it again he was going to thrash him. I jumped out of my bedroll and walked over to him. I told him to be quiet, but he just ignored me and continued cursing at the other man. I grabbed him by the shoulders and shook him, but he just kept running his mouth.

Up to this point, nobody had challenged my authority as squad leader, but I felt like Corporal Mooring was being deliberately disrespectful to me and the other members of the squad. The moment of truth had arrived, and I felt like I needed to do something. So I slapped him on the side of the head and knocked him back into a corner.

I stood over him and told him that he should never talk that way about anybody in our squad or the entire U.S. Army. He gave me a dumfounded stare and immediately apologized to me and the rest of the squad. He assured us all that it would never happen again, and he was true to his word. I never had a minute's trouble with that man for the rest of our tour in Europe.

I took a bit of a hard line when it came to discipline in my squad. If the Army made a rule about it, we tried to follow that rule as best we could. I wasn't really afraid of losing control of the men, but I felt that discipline was the only way to get a job done safely and successfully. If the men knew that I was watching and concerned about their welfare, they would be more likely to take pride in their work and do it well. Also, if they were used to following orders, then when the heat was on in combat, they would concentrate on their jobs and not question why they were doing something a certain way. I approached discipline as a necessity for order and safety, and I tried to administer it as fairly as possible.

There was a young man of Polish descent who came from Pennsylvania. His name was Tumabayski, and he was a heavy-set boy who was the laziest man in my squad. He would always follow orders, but sometimes he did it on his own schedule. I remember that he contacted me after the War and told me that he had been turned down for disability benefits by the government. He wondered if I would write a letter for him stating that he had been injured in the War and should be granted disability. The only catch was that he hadn't been injured in the War. I wrote him back and told him that I wouldn't feel comfortable making such a claim, and I never heard from him again.

As a leader, I wasn't supposed to have favorites, but sometimes the boss can't help but like the ones who work the hardest and do the best job. That's the way I felt about Corporals Rupert and Bosic. They were both from the same small town in Pennsylvania, and they were two of the most conscientious soldiers I came across in the Army. They would do even the dirtiest job without one word of complaint.

Rupert was the clown of the squad. Out of the blue, he would walk up to me or another member of the squad and say, "Tell me the truth and don't tell me no lies. Which do you love the best, your Momma or your Poppa?" He was always quick with a joke, but he and Bosic sure were the type of men I wanted beside me in a foxhole with the enemy close by.

I don't know what the other squads were like, but I'd guess that ours was pretty typical. We were all just young men far from home trying our best to do our jobs and stay alive. I was a little partial, though. We may have been similar to all the others, but I always felt that my squad was just a little bit better.

I kept in touch with some of the boys by mail shortly after we returned to the States, but after a little while we all got wrapped up in our civilian lives and stopped writing. That seems to be the way life is. We each run in our own little circles, and if your circle doesn't intersect another's circle, you just lose touch. But I'll always be grateful for the wonderful job my squad did, and each one will always have a special place in my heart. And in my mind they'll remain forever young when I recall the joys and sorrows we shared in the greatest adventure of our lives.

32

We were constantly on the move once the Germans started retreating, and one morning we were awakened by a phone call from headquarters. The company first sergeant, who had a penchant for remaining at or near headquarters whenever we were on the front lines and danger was near, informed us that the Germans who occupied the town across the river had moved out during the night, and we were being transported to another area to catch up with our assigned infantry battalion. As day was breaking, a thick fog rolled in off the river, and we could barely see a few feet in front of us as we loaded into trucks for the three- or four-mile trip back to headquarters.

We had to travel through a dense wooded area on the road to headquarters, and apparently the Germans hadn't retreated quite as far as we thought. When they heard the roars of the truck engines as we crawled along the road, they opened up on us with everything they had. Because of the dense fog, they couldn't see us, so they just fired blindly in the direction of the motor noises. Mortar shells started falling all around us, and machine gun bullets whizzed around and through our trucks.

I was riding on the passenger side in the lead truck, and I heard a machine gun bullet strike the door just below my legs, pass through the cab, and exit out the door beside the driver. I was hunched over in my seat trying to make myself as small as possible, and I had no idea how close a call this blind shot had been until we stopped several hundred yards later, once we had cleared the danger. That bullet had missed my legs by just an inch or two as it blasted through the cab, and it had come equally close to the driver. If it had hit my legs, it would surely have splintered any bones it hit, inflicting who knows what type of permanent damage.

I had many close calls like that one, and I often didn't realize it until the danger had passed, but the Lord had to have his hand on me throughout the War. There were so many times, like that one, where only Divine intervention could explain my deliverance. Sure, I was careful and didn't try to be a hero, and I was well trained and conscientious about my duties, but there were just situations where the Lord seemed to build a wall of protection around me that prevented harm from coming my way. My mother was a strong believer in the power of prayer, and I know she prayed diligently for me every day I was away in the Army. And I can't help but think that the Lord heard her prayers and brought me home safely.

33

As the Germans retreated across their homeland, they tried to make life as difficult as they could for their pursuers. Any obstacle they could leave in the path of the Allies bought that much more time they could use to fortify the remaining constricted territory they had to defend. So, they blew bridges over every ravine and stream as they gave up each inch of their precious land. As we chased them, most of our work as Combat Engineers was spent bridging these obstacles.

We used Bailey bridges to span many small streams and ravines, and these metal bridges were quick and easy to install, and they proved to be very durable and sturdy. But for the larger rivers, we had to construct more permanent bridges that could withstand the rigors of near constant foot and motorized vehicle traffic, as well as attacks by the Germans.

The bridge that we constructed over the beautiful Danube River was just such a span. The original bridge was made of metal built on concrete piers, but German demolition and Allied bombing had left it nothing more than a twisted mass of scrap at the bottom of the river. We rebuilt it using wood.

The German countryside was filled with commercial and private sawmills. The German people took great pride in their workmanship with wood, as evidenced by the beautiful decorations and furnishings we found in homes all across the country. The men who owned and operated these sawmills were extremely protective of their operations, and they didn't take too kindly to the American Engineers who pulled up in their Army trucks.

They never actually fired at us, but they often had to be escorted away at gunpoint before they would give up their inventory or equipment. We never had to shoot any of these civilians, but we sometimes had to physically remove them before we could get the lumber, logs, and other wood products that we required for our construction projects.

Since most of the concrete pillars that formed the base of the bridge had been destroyed, we replaced them with log pilings that were driven into the riverbed. These pilings were twelve to eighteen inches in diameter and perhaps forty or fifty feet long. They were huge pieces of timber that were flat on the top end and pointed on the end that was driven into the riverbed.

We scoured the area sawmills for these pilings, and sometimes we had to use the equipment at the sawmills to cut them for ourselves. I recall one commercial sawmill that had what was called an up-and-down saw that was powered by a big diesel generator. Instead of the typical round saw blade that cut through the wood in a circular motion, this mill had two blades that moved up and down in a true sawing motion. We simply aligned the wood with those blades and set them to a specific width, and they cut the wood to the desired width on both sides, cutting the work in half. It was quite an in-genious set-up, the only one I've ever seen of its type.

We had a pole trailer that we pulled behind a 2½-ton truck to move the pilings. We placed them part on the trailer with the other part resting on the back of the truck when we hauled them, and we loaded them with an Army crane. Our operation resembled a modern (for the times) construction site with nothing but the best and most expensive equipment utilized.

We obviously couldn't drive these pilings into the bedrock by hand, so we used a machine called a pile driver to do the job. A pile driver was a piece of heavy equipment that resembled a large crane. It had arms that extended from the front that clamped onto the pil-ing to hold it in place until it was driven far enough into the ground to stand on its own.

The crane had a heavy-duty cable with a huge, flat piece of steel, called the driver, attached to it. We placed a metal cap over the end of the piling to keep it from splitting when we used the driver. The crane would retract the driver twenty-five or thirty feet above the piling and then release it. The driver would slam into the top of the piling with a ringing clank, driving it into the ground. I was familiar with a pile driver from my days working on the B&O. We used a similar piece of machinery to build several railroad tressels along the line from Green Spring to Petersburg.

One morning shortly after we started the bridge across the Danube, the man who ran the crane that loaded the pilings on the trailers didn't show up for work. The captain asked if anyone knew of his where-abouts, and a man in my squad said that the operator had reported to sick call that morning and wouldn't be coming to work.

The captain asked desperately if anyone else in the company had ever run a crane before. He was greeted with stone silence from his men. This time almost pleading, because I suppose he was getting heat from the infantry divisions that were waiting to cross the river when we finished the bridge, he asked again if anyone thought they would like to at least give it a try. I hesitated, but I finally stepped forward and volunteered.

I climbed into the cab and looked over all the knobs and levers that regulated the crane's movements, and I instantly wondered what I had gotten myself into. I fiddled and experimented for several minutes, pulling a lever or knob and then watching the results. After a while I was emboldened to move the crane forward and attempt to pick up and load one of those huge logs. I was clumsy and overly cautious at first, but as I became more aware of the machine's movements I started to get more comfortable. I'm not going to say that I was as good as the original operator, but we did make progress on the bridge that day, although not nearly as much as we would have if the regular operator hadn't been sick.

We used wooden girders to form the base of the bridge, and the floor was constructed of 3"x 6" wood planks that were fifteen feet long. We got as many of these planks as we could find from local sawmills, and when we ran out we had to cut more ourselves from the wood supplies at the mills. We fastened the planks down with 60-penny spikes, which were about nine inches long and a half of an inch in diameter.

I mentioned before that we had the most modern equipment of the times at our disposal, and that was never more evident than when we nailed down the planks for the floor of the bridge. It would have taken us forever to drive in all those spikes by hand using hammers, so the Army provided a heavy-duty nail gun to do the job. An air compressor mounted on the back of our truck powered the gun. The compressor carried 100 pounds of pressure, and when we squeezed the trigger on that nail gun those spikes instantly sank all the way into the planks in one motion. It was a marvel to watch those nail guns in action.

We worked around the clock for seven days before we finally completed the bridge across the Danube. We set up huge spotlights that illuminated the area like daylight so we could work at night. Of course, the Germans weren't that far away, and they loved to sneak into range and fire a few 88's at us while we worked. But our infantry and artillery did a pretty good job of holding the enemy at bay while we worked, and the men and the bridge escaped unscathed the entire time we were there.

I felt a great sense of pride when the first units of armor and infantry rolled across the Danube. We all considered each of these projects to be one more step closer to ending the War and returning home, a thought that kept us going through the endless hours of hard work.

34

Our relentless march continued across the German homeland, and this time the Combat Engineers were at or near the front all the time. Whenever the infantry encountered a gully, stream, or river, the Engineers had to be handy to bridge the obstacle. We built several Bailey bridges and many more out of wood for longer spans.

We knew that we had to clear one more major geographic obstacle before we could advance into the very heart of Germany. This obstacle was the Rhine River, which generals from both sides hailed as the final natural fortress in the War. In preparation for bridging the river, we started hauling supplies and material four weeks in advance of the actual construction. We hid these supplies near the projected point of crossing under camouflage nets in wooded areas until the time came to actually use them in building a bridge across the Rhine.

We moved most of these supplies at night so the Germans wouldn't know what we were up to. We traveled in convoys using what we called nightlights on our trucks. These nightlights were covers that we placed over the headlights and taillights of our trucks that only allowed a small beam of light to shine through (we called them "cat eyes"), just enough that the lead truck could see a few feet in front. Every other truck in the convoy followed the one in front of it. We had to stay pretty close together, roughly twenty-five or thirty feet apart, because these "cat eyes" were only visible at close range.

On one of our deliveries, the truck that my driver and I were following made a wrong turn, and somehow we stayed on the right road, but we weren't close enough to keep contact since the truck immediately in front of us was no longer there. We came to a crossroads and I thought I remembered the correct turn to make, but in the darkness I was completely confused. We branched off on the wrong road and headed right into a roadblock.

This turned out to be a good news/bad news situation. The good news was that Americans were manning the roadblock. The bad news was that these Americans were part of the First Cavalry Division. Not only was the First Cavalry an elite, well-trained outfit, but it also appeared that they were quite suspicious by nature.

They stopped our truck and told us to get out. They first asked for the password for the day, which was trouble for us because we departed on our run before that day's password had been given out. We told them that, but they weren't convinced. They took us to their headquarters and had us empty everything out of our pockets. We took off our coats, and they went through every pocket and crevice in them, trying to find any shred of evidence showing that we were Germans. They asked us a series of questions about everything from what unit we were from to who had won the World Series the year before. It seemed like no answer was good enough for them. They were absolutely convinced that we were spies trying to infiltrate their position.

After several minutes of this intense interrogation, I finally started to lose my patience, since nothing we said seemed to convince them. I told them exactly where my unit was located and suggested that they radio back to the 1258th Engineers to verify the information I was giving them. After several minutes of wrangling with my unit, the guards let us through at last. We proceeded to our destination and dropped off our load, and when we finally returned to our camp it was daylight. I was frustrated with the way the First Cavalry treated us, but with all the enemy intrigue that had been going around, I guess I really couldn't blame them all that much.

We operated on the assumption that the Germans wouldn't possibly leave any bridge standing across the Rhine, but the Allies were handed a special gift early in 1945. On March 7, lead elements of the U.S. Ninth Armored Division rolled onto the heights overlooking the small German town of Remagen. To their surprise, they saw that the Ludendorff Bridge, a railroad bridge that spanned the Rhine, was still intact, and elements of the German infantry were retreating across it.

Immediately sensing the importance of this discovery, the Ninth Armored swooped down on the town and the bridge in an effort to capture the span before the Germans could destroy it. Despite the Germans' best efforts to blow it up before retreating, the bridge stood for ten days before collapsing into the cold waters of the Rhine. During those ten days, Allied troops flooded across the bridge and established a foothold on the west bank that held despite desperate German attempts to wipe it out. The entire incident is often referred to as the "Miracle of Remagen."

Even before the Ludendorff Bridge collapsed, we began building a pontoon bridge about a half a mile downstream. The brass realized that the Ludendorff Bridge could fall at any time, and the steady stream of soldiers and equipment that had begun to roll over the Rhine had to continue uninterrupted if the Allies were to maintain and expand the foothold they had established on the other side.

Two different Combat Engineer battalions worked on the bridge around the clock. Headquarters decided that a wooden bridge would take too long to build over such a long span, so we settled on a pontoon bridge. I mentioned earlier that bridge building technology hadn't kept up with advances in the size and weight of tanks and other vehicles of war, but some improvements had been made in the strength and endurance of pontoon bridges as the War progressed. We could only hope that these improvements would hold up under the heavy strain of foot and vehicle traffic necessary to eliminate the last bastions of German resistance.

The pontoons that we used were like inflatable boats made of thick rubber, and they were about thirty feet long and eight feet wide. I'm not sure if the rubber was actually thick enough to resist puncture when hit with a rifle or machine gun bullet, but none of the pontoons ruptured while we worked with them under battle conditions. We inflated the pontoons with the big air compressors that we carried on the back of our trucks.

Before we floated the pontoons on the river, we had to have some way to keep them in place. Using a flat-bottomed barge equipped with a heavy-duty crane, we dropped anchors that very much resembled the ones used on big naval ships about fifty yards upstream from the spot where we wanted to build the bridge. Attached to these anchors were two heavy cables that we used to keep two pontoons in place. We picked out a spot where the current wasn't too swift, and those anchors did a surprisingly good job of maintaining the position of the pontoons. The Rhine was nearly 1,000 feet wide at the point where we were building the bridge, so several pontoons and anchors were needed to complete the project.

The pontoons were made of durable rubber, but they weren't thick enough to withstand the constant wear that tank tracks and truck wheels would present. To protect the pontoons, we laid two steel tracks that were twenty feet long and two feet wide atop the pontoons. The sections of tracks were held together with steel pins that allowed them to swivel as a tank or truck crossed, pushing the pontoons down into the water.

The enemy seldom missed a chance to take a shot as us while we were building that bridge. As had been the case when we bridged the Danube, work carried on twenty-four hours a day on the span over the Rhine. When our work first started, the German attacks were nothing more than a nuisance, because they couldn't really get close enough to us to be very accurate. If they did hit one of the Engineers, it was more luck than anything else.

They especially liked to attack at night, when they were cloaked in darkness while all the workers on the bridge were silhouetted against the bright lights that we employed so our work could continue after dark. The Germans knew that the Allied forces on their side of the river were concentrated in one relatively small area to guard against counter attacks that could endanger their tenuous hold on the west bank. So, they were emboldened to come right down to the edge of the river to fire at us.

As our work progressed toward the far shore, those attacks that had been nothing more than an inconvenience now turned into a real threat. We were required to carry our weapons with us while we worked on the bridge, but we really didn't have the time or the inclination to stop working and get into a firefight with the enemy. Rather, we relied on the support that the infantry on our side could provide, and for the most part they did a pretty good job. But the constant threat of enemy attacks wore on our frazzled nerves as the bridge neared completion and the sleepless nights mounted.

After the Ludendorff Bridge toppled into the river, the sense of urgency to complete our bridge increased quite a bit. The Army realized that we could work faster if the threat of attack was reduced somewhat, so they contacted the Army Air Corps for help. The Air Corps dropped paratroopers on the far shore to drive the Germans back away from the river and lessen the possibility of attack. We still received scattered small arms fire, especially at night, but for the most part we worked in relative safety from that point forward.

But the work was painfully slow. Getting the barges to drop the anchors in precisely the right spots became harder the farther we progressed from the shore. Inflating and then floating the pontoons into place was slow, tedious work as well. Getting the barge in position so the crane could place the tracks on the pontoons in exactly the proper place was time consuming, and aligning the tracks so they could be pinned together was very difficult as the pontoons bobbed up and down on the river's current. And having armored platoons revving their engines in eager anticipation of our completing the task didn't help all that much either.

After nearly a month of round-the-clock work by two different Engineer battalions, the end was in sight at last. All told, the bridge covered 997 feet, the second-longest pontoon bridge ever built across the Rhine by just twenty-five feet. As we completed the run-up on both sides of the river, General Patton's tanks lined up for miles in eager anticipation of the crossing. By this time March had turned into April, and General Patton was itching to deliver the death knell to the Third Reich.

When we finally finished the bridge, we stood on the bank as the first units of tanks prepared to roll across. I didn't see how those pontoons could hold up under the pressure of a sixty-ton tank, but the men driving those tanks didn't seem worried at all. They rolled up the run-up to the bridge and started across. As a tank would run over each pontoon, that section of the bridge would sink until the water covered halfway up the tracks on the tank. But as the tank moved on to the next pontoon, the previous one would pop to the surface, ready to take on the next vehicle. It seemed that no punishment was too harsh for that incredible invention.

A lot of maintenance was required to keep the bridge passable. We were constantly checking the pins that held the sections of track together, because the repeated up-and-down motion as vehicles crossed put tremendous strain on them. We also had to grease the pins to be sure that they continued to swivel properly. We continually checked the air pressure in the pontoons. They had to be filled to capacity at all times to ensure they could carry the weight of all the tanks and trucks that crossed the bridge.

Our company maintained the bridge for about two weeks after we finished building it before we were relieved by another company and moved on to our next assignment. I still think back with pride that I worked on that span over the Rhine. At the time I could only see that the bridge just brought us one step closer to home.

35

As we raced across the German countryside in pursuit of the Nazis, we came in close contact with many civilians. We found the German people and lifestyle quite similar to those in our own country. They were simple folks who were caught up in a conflict mostly not of their own design. Their homes and lives had been shattered by the six years of the War, and frankly they seemed relieved when the Allied forces rolled through their towns.

Most of the towns we passed through had narrow streets with houses lining them on both sides. These dwellings were crowded together and came right up to the street. Whenever a body of Allied troops and vehicles passed through one of these towns, the citizens would line the streets and hang out of second-story windows, waving American flags (I have no clue where all those flags came from) and shouting greetings to the troops. They laughed and yelled as though they were relieved that they had finally been liberated from their own government.

Many of the civilians that I talked to complained of the harsh treatment they had suffered under Hitler's regime. They told stories of deprivation and ruthless invasions of privacy. They told how they always felt their own government was watching them for the slightest show of disobedience or complaint, which was greeted with instant punishment. But I think the thing they were most happy about was that the War was finally over for them.

With the arrival of the Allies, they no longer had to worry about bombing or shelling. They no longer had to worry about soldiers hiding in and fighting from their homes. They no longer had to cower in basements or shelters while a battle raged above them. And best of all, they no longer had to fear for the lives of their loved ones.

We in the U.S. were lucky in one sense during the War. We soldiers had to risk our lives daily, but at least we knew that our families were safe at home. The Germans, and millions of others in Europe, lived on the battlefields of World War II. They saw the horror and devastation of war out their living room windows. After six years of armed conflict, the last two of which had been a particular nightmare as the bombing and fighting reached further into the German homeland, they were ready to start their lives over with the few possessions they had salvaged and face what the future had in store for them.

We entered one German town near dark, and an elderly couple greeted us and invited my whole squad into their home. They had moved all their furniture into one room, leaving their living room empty. We threw down our bedrolls on the floor and prepared for a good night's sleep, a luxury we hadn't enjoyed very much over the past few weeks.

The man and his wife entered the room and asked if we would like some refreshments before turning in. They said they knew we had been living off rations for several weeks, and they thought we might like a change of pace. We really had no idea what they had in mind, but I told them that we would love something to eat and drink.

They disappeared into the kitchen, and a few minutes later they came back with several bottles of wine, a huge roll of homemade cheese, and several packages of crackers. We pounced on these delicacies, especially the wine. We were a squad of dirty, smelly foreigners who had invaded their home for the night, but they were so grateful to the Allies for liberating them from their own leaders that they opened their home and their pantry to us.

I hated the Nazis for the death and destruction they had caused all over the world. I hated them for starting a war that killed and wounded so many of the friends I had made in the Army. I hated them because I had to travel halfway around the world and fight in that war. I hated them because they opposed everything that I valued, our very existence.

But I couldn't hate the German people. I've never run for a political office, and I don't know how relations between governments work, but I just couldn't blame those people I met, the common Germans, for the mess their government had created. I actually felt sorry for them, because I couldn't help but think that all the events leading up to the War and the subsequent fighting had been completely beyond their control. They were like pawns in a chess game that their leaders had manipulated and sacrificed for a set of false ideals. They were far too much like Americans to ever hate.

Apparently not all Allied soldiers shared my warm feelings for the German people. When many of the GI's entered a home, they went there for one reason, to see what they could steal. Anything of value, either real or perceived, was fair game to these looters. All sense of right and wrong seemed to go out the window during the War.

Many held the opinion that the Germans had started the War, and one way to repay them for that mistake was to rob them blind. Soldiers took guns, silverware, jewelry, money, and anything else they thought was valuable. But they were often disappointed when it came time to return to the U.S. Most of the time the Army confiscated these treasures before the soldiers got on the ship to return home.

36

As the month of April progressed, it became evident that the War was coming to a close. The American and British Armies in the East and the Russians in the West had the German army in a deadly vice, and the distance between the two Allied forces decreased with each passing day.

The soldiers in every engineer and infantry platoon were starting to talk about the end of the War, and everyone became extra cautious when carrying out his duties because we all felt that our lives would be wasted if we got killed now, after the outcome of the War had been decided. But we still had our duties to perform because the Nazis had not yet capitulated, so it was a very awkward time as we tried to stay as much out of harm's way as we could while still obeying the orders that our commanders issued.

Even without a formal surrender, we all knew that the end was inevitable. We saw thousands of German soldiers marching away from the front lines every day. They were technically prisoners of war, but they were surrendering so quickly that the Allies simply couldn't round them all up fast enough. Most of the Germans had thrown down or lost their weapons, so they weren't really a threat to us. They willingly marched without a fight toward prison camps that the Army had built at various points in Germany.

Most of the large groups of prisoners that we passed had just a skeleton crew of Allied soldiers guarding them, and some had no guards at all. They marched along with their heads down, averting the eyes of the Allied soldiers as if they were somehow disgraced by their defeat. We didn't regard them in that light at all. We thought they had been brave, resourceful fighters who had defended their homeland gallantly. Just because their government had led them deceitfully and disgracefully into this global conflict in no way diminished the respect that we held for the average German soldier. After suffering their second crushing defeat in the last thirty years, though, I could see how the Germans would feel a little inferior, especially after they had come so close to dominating nearly the entire world earlier in the War.

Word reached my unit a couple of days after the fact that Hitler had committed suicide on April 30, but his death didn't seem to have as much impact on the fighting as we had hoped. Battles still raged, and brave men still died even after Germany's leader had taken the coward's way out of the mess he and his henchmen had created.

A day or so after we heard the news about Hitler's death, my company moved into the vicinity of Heidelberg, which was located on the west bank of the Rhine, to work on more bridge-building projects. There was still intense fighting in the area, as the German units there obviously hadn't heard that they were fighting for a hopeless cause. After a day or two we turned from Engineers to infantry when the word circulated that the Germans were massing for a big counter-attack on the town, but those reports turned out to be false.

It was early in the morning of May 8, 1945, and several of the members of my squad and I were standing around a fire barrel for warmth. To make a fire barrel, we found an empty 55-gallon drum and poured in five gallons of gasoline from a Jerrycan. When we dropped in a match, there was a pretty intense explosion, but eventually the fire settled into a steady simmer that would keep a group of five or six soldiers warm for thirty or forty minutes before we had to add more fuel.

We sometimes joked that gas was rationed and in very short supply back in the U.S., and we were burning it in Germany to stay warm. I know my father would have dearly loved to have those five gallons of gasoline that we were burning at that very moment.

Suddenly, one of the members of my squad appeared with a stack of papers under his arm and a broad smile on his face. He handed each of us standing around the fire a copy of the Army newspaper Stars and Stripes. Across the front blared the huge, bold-faced headline, " VICTORY." We read the article under that headline and found that German General Jodl had signed the official surrender papers the day before, and this day, May 8, was officially declared as VE Day, for Victory in Europe.

All kinds of thoughts and emotions flooded through my mind as I read about the day that all of us had longed for since we first heard about Hitler and the Nazis six years before. I thought of home and how great it would be to finally see my family and friends again. I thought of the men in my squad and how lucky I had been to have such great soldiers under my command, and also how lucky we had been to survive the War.

I also thought about the brave men who wouldn't be returning home, the ones who had made the ultimate sacrifice for a country that they loved and believed in. Images of the horror and devastation that I had witnessed in my six months of combat came flooding back to me. I saw the faces of the German children as they begged us for food or scampered away as bombs and mortar shells crashed down around them.

I recalled a scene that I witnessed several weeks before, when we first entered the Saar Valley with General Patton's Army. We were trying to catch up with the infantry to complete some engineering task when we came across a country road where General Patton's armored division had recently passed. The carnage I witnessed there will stay with me as long as I live.

All along the road for perhaps ten miles were the mutilated carcasses of horses that had been strafed by U.S. P-51 Mustang fighters. The P-51's had opened up with their 20mm canons on this column of animals that were pulling ammunition wagons for the Germans. Between the shells from the airplanes and the explosions of the ammunition as it went up, not much was left of those horses. I had loved and worked with horses since I was a little boy, and it grieved me to see those animals wasted in war.

But what I saw on the other side of the road grieved me even more. There was a big open field that had recently been cleared by a German farmer. The stumps from the trees that he had cut were scattered around the field. This field had been the scene of a deadly infantry battle just hours before, and soldiers from both sides were strewn all over the place.

I gazed at the twisted, mutilated bodies of those brave men and wondered why they had been the ones chosen for death and not me. They had families and friends back home who would grieve when they learned of their death, just as mine would have. Why them, and not me? That was a question that I asked myself not only on VE Day but many times after I got back home.

I quickly snapped back to the present, and to the joy and relief that I felt that this horrible ordeal was finally coming to an end. I knew that I still had many dangerous situations to face before I saw my family at home, but for now I was relieved that the fighting was finally over.

Part Four:
Occupation

37

When the War ended, naturally all our thoughts turned to home and how soon we would get there. But the Army had other ideas in mind. Obviously, all the troops couldn't go home at the same time because there wasn't adequate transportation to handle all those people at once, and Europeans, especially the Germans, needed help to put their broken homes and lives back together again.

So, the Army devised a plan to alleviate both problems. That's when the word "points" entered our vocabulary. The Army set up a system that would reward those who had served the longest and bring relief to those who were needed the most at home. Soldiers earned points in four different categories: time in the Service, time spent overseas, combat awards, and fathers of children under eighteen back in the States.

We earned one point apiece for each month we spent in the service and overseas. We received five points for each medal we earned and each major battle we fought in. Men earned twelve points for each child they had at home under eighteen, up to three children. The magic number was 85. That's how many points we had to accumulate to earn our way back to America.

Our most cherished possessions quickly became our Adjusted Service Rating Cards. These were the records that were tabulated by the various company clerks that told up to the minute exactly how many points each soldier had accumulated. Men were constantly bothering the clerks to check up on their points and trying to figure out a way to drive up the totals on those cards, usually to no avail.

Many of the veteran soldiers who had served in several different theaters of war loaded on ships and headed home just a few days after the armistice was signed. They had done their time and deserved to be the first to go home. But others, me included, still had quite a bit of work to do. As near as I could figure it, when the War ended I was a little over halfway home.

I had been in the service 22 months, eight of which I'd spent overseas, for a total of 30 points. I'd fought in three major battles (Battle of the Bulge, Crossing the Rhine, and Central Europe) for a total of 15 points. I came up a little short in the children department, though. All told, I had 45 points, 40 short of the total I needed to get home. Even earning double points each month, I was still looking at quite an extended stay in Europe before sitting in front of the home fires once more.

Army life really wasn't all the bad, especially since nobody was trying to kill me every day. I had pretty good food and clothes and a comfortable place to live. I was in a part of the world that I likely would never have another chance to visit. I was doing interesting work that really helped out the German people. Except for not seeing my family for almost two years, there were lots worse situations that a twenty-one-year-old could find himself in. So, I did my job each day and tried to make the best of the situation, just as I had done every other day while I was in the Army.

Way back when I was taking my Basic Training, I mentioned that I really had no idea what combat would be like, and I referred to my state with the old saying, "Ignorance is bliss." Little did I know how much that axiom applied to me once again when I received my first assignment after the War.

After the End-of-War Celebration was over, we turned from a fighting Army into an occupation Army. Our job was to help the very people who had been shooting at us just a few days before. And boy, did they ever need our help!

The German homeland, at least in and around Heidelberg where I was stationed, was a mess. Roads and bridges were blown to bits. Houses and other buildings were in shambles. Railroads were inoperable as Allied bombing had concentrated on that form of transportation to cripple movements of troops and precious supplies. There really was no government, other than the U.S. Army, because all the buildings where the government previously worked lay in piles of rubble throughout the city. As Engineers, our job was to help the citizens rebuild their land so that they could move forward with a somewhat brighter future.

But we wouldn't be helping those in the Heidelberg vicinity. Just a couple of weeks after the armistice, sometime near the beginning of June, my battalion boarded a troop train for the journey north to the port city of Antwerp, Belgium. We were told that our Engineers would be working to repair the port facilities so that desperately needed supplies for the civilians and the Army could arrive through there.

Our main focus was on the railroads that led to and from the port. Allied bombs had devastated the railroads, leaving most of the tracks a twisted mess of metal and wood. The work we were doing was very similar to the jobs we had performed during the War, except that those who had been shooting at us were the ones working side-by-side with us now. German prisoners, who had yet to be released to go home, performed most of the labor on the railroads.

We worked on the railroads for over two months, never knowing what the Army actually had in mind for us. We knew that other units had either shipped out or were preparing to ship out for the War in Japan, which, although the outcome was no longer in doubt, still raged across the Pacific. We had no idea that our battalion had been sent to Antwerp so that we would be close to our point of departure because we were next on the list to ship out for the Pacific Theater.

Once more luck or fate or Divine intervention (whatever name you want to give to it) stepped in. On August 6, 1945, President Truman gave the word to drop the first atomic bomb ever used in combat on the Japanese city Hiroshima. Three days later, a second atomic bomb was dropped on Nagasaki. On August 14, Emperor Hirohito cabled Japan's surrender to President Truman, and the following day the announcement was made to the entire world that World War II was finally over.

Shortly after the armistice was signed aboard the USS Missouri in Tokyo Bay on September 2, our company commander told us how close we had come to shipping out for Japan. He said that the orders had been issued, and we were just waiting for the ship to arrive that would have carried us to the Pacific Theater.

I'm not really sure where I stand on using nuclear weapons in war, but I have to admit that I was very happy that President Truman had decided to use them on that occasion. Even though I was committed to several more months in the Military, I felt a tremendous sense of relief in knowing that at least I wouldn't have to spend that time in places where hostile troops would be shooting at me.

38

Shortly after VJ Day, we loaded on a train and shipped back to Germany. Our assignment was road repair and construction. Allied bombing had left the German highway system in a shambles. Bridges had been wiped out, and large sections of highway, especially near the larger cities, were nothing more than pockmarked wastelands.

Our job was to repair the bridges over streams and gullies and try to make the roads passable. Most of our work was done near Frankfurt, and we even got to see and work on the world famous Autobahn.

The Autobahn was a construction marvel for the times. Construction began in the 1920's, long before Hitler and the Nazis came to power, but like all things that proved useful during his regime, Hitler took credit for it. When the Nazis came to power in 1933, Hitler could see the economic, military, and propaganda benefits of the Autobahn, so he committed masses of slave labor to its construction.

The Autobahn may have benefited the economy and the propaganda efforts, but it did very little for the War effort. Since more troops and materials could be crammed into boxcars than trucks, railroads were the prime movers of the military during the War. Also, tank and truck traffic quickly destroyed the primitive surface that was used on the Autobahn. As the War dragged on, construction ceased because all that slave labor was needed to make bullets and bombs. As a result, large stretches of the Autobahn were incomplete, further hampering the movement of military personnel and supplies.

But now the War was over, and the U.S. Military, as well as the German civilians, needed roads to transport food and supplies to major urban areas, and this super highway had originally been built for just that purpose. Using mostly German prisoners, we spent endless hours hauling and shoveling rocks and gravel to fill the massive holes in the pavement. It seemed that every culvert and bridge had either been bombed or blown up with explosives, so we spent countless hours hauling materials and building back bridges to span those obstacles. After a while I started to feel like I was back in civilian life. I had a regular job, much like the one I had on the B&O, and I just got up every morning and went to work.

But sometimes my Engineer Company reverted back to its infantry roots. Even though the War was officially over and all hostilities should have ended, there were several fanatical groups of German soldiers who simply refused to give up. Among those groups were the German SS troops, who had been the most elite soldiers in Hitler's Third Reich. They had been brainwashed to such an extent that they couldn't fathom that Germany had surrendered. They apparently thought that the whole surrender thing was a ruse to buy time for the Nazis. They felt that it was still their duty to kill as many Allied soldiers as they could.

The Army knew that these fanatics had to be stopped, and eventually I was part of the outfit assigned to stop them. One tactic that the SS used was to fake a wound so they would be admitted to a hospital. Since many of the hospitals were crammed to overflowing with real wounded soldiers and civilians, some of these SS men were often moved to hotels in the larger cities until they recuperated.

Somehow they would retain or gain access to their weapons, and they had the habit of shooting at Allied soldiers as they went about their business in the cities. Several Allied men had been wounded and killed by these guerrilla tactics. To remedy this situation, the Army decided to round up all these supposedly wounded SS men and haul them to prison camps for safe keeping. My company drew the duty of going to the hospitals and hotels and rounding them up.

We were stationed near the town of Regensburg at the time, and I have to admit that the old feelings of tension and anxiety that I had felt before the armistice began to surface again as we moved from building to building, not knowing exactly what we would run into when we entered a hospital or hotel room.

When we walked into a room, we always had our weapons at the ready, and for the most part the SS troopers went peacefully once they saw they had no other choice. We rounded up several hundred of these soldiers as we swept through the city, and I couldn't believe that the Army had let that many dangerous fugitives slip through the cracks.

I recall one incident involving an SS colonel. When I entered the hotel room in which he was staying, I found this elderly soldier sitting on the edge of his bed, dressed in his military uniform. I explained to him that he needed to come with me to a detainment camp. At first he acted as if he didn't understand what I was telling him to do. When I finally got the message over to him, he seemed offended that I wanted to take him away to be housed with the other common soldiers. As I said before, these SS men were used to preferential treatment, and the idea of associating with enlisted men or draftees was most repulsive to them.

He reached under his bed and removed a small satchel. I leveled my weapon at him and told him to open it slowly. He unzipped the satchel, and I could see a long knife inside. I told him to remove the knife, and it turned out to be a silver bayonet that had been issued to all the SS officers. I told him to hand the bayonet to me, and he refused. I asked him once more, and this time I clicked the safety off on my rifle. I'm not sure if I actually would have shot him had he not followed my instructions, but thankfully he handed the bayonet over to me. I still have it today among my souvenirs from the War.

After we brought the SS soldiers outside, my men would search each one and take all his possessions, including watches, rings, and other jewelry, away from him. Most of the time the men would keep or sell these valuables. I guess we figured that all those things would be confiscated before they entered the prison camps anyway, so we might as well get them rather than somebody else. I brought home a fine pocket watch that we took from an SS officer on one of these sweeps. I gave it to my father, and he carried it with him for several years.

After the search, we crammed the SS soldiers onto troop trucks for transportation to the prisons. These trucks had seats that folded down on both sides of the bed, but we kept the seats folded up so we could get more men on the truck for each trip. We herded them on like cattle, not even giving them enough room to turn around, let alone sit down.

I mentioned before that I had great respect for the common German soldier, but those feelings didn't extend to the SS men. These troops had committed some of the most heinous crimes of the War, and I had little or no sympathy for them. If they were uncomfortable during the ride or inside the prison camps, then I felt that they were getting what they deserved.

Conditions at these prison camps were less than ideal. The one near Regensburg where we took most of our prisoners was nothing more than an open field that contained several hundred acres. The compound was surrounded by razor wire to discourage escapes. There were no barracks or other buildings for shelter. The prisoners slept in the one-man tents that they had used in combat. Their meals were the same rations that the American soldiers ate while in the field, and they got their water from a large tank centrally located in the compound. I'm sure that those SS men were shocked to be placed in such conditions, but as I said before, we felt like they were getting what they deserved.

We received reports that civilians were taking shots at American soldiers, so orders came down from headquarters that we were to search every house in town and confiscate all the weapons and ammunition that we found. Once more, I felt quite uncomfortable walking into those homes, never knowing if we would be greeted with a smile or a gunshot. Our search collected some of the most beautiful and unusual weapons I'd ever seen. We loaded these guns on our truck and dumped them off in a huge pile in front of headquarters. I don't know what ever became of all those guns, but I sure would have loved to bring some of them home with me.

I could possibly have concealed some of the weapons and tried to bring them back to the U.S., but we were thoroughly searched, both our person and all our belongings, before we boarded our ship, and any firearms that we had were confiscated. The officers were authorized to bring back some souvenirs, including guns and other valuables, but the common soldiers were not afforded that luxury.

I did manage to get one gun home, however. During our sweep through Belgium, we were starting to run short on ammunition for our M-1's, but I noticed that many German rifles, which were the 8mm Mauser, were scattered over the battlefield after the enemy retreated. I picked one up and found it to my liking.

The sling was on the side of the weapon, which allowed it to rest flat on my back. The M-1 had the sling on the front, and the trigger guard always dug into my back when I marched long distances. Ammunition was plentiful for the 8mm because nearly all the German small arms, machine guns included, fired the same ammunition. Whenever I ran short on ammo, I just stopped by an abandoned machine gun nest and picked up a fresh supply.

I loved that rifle and determined to try to get it back to the States. I was told that the only way I could get it home was through the mail. I had to cut a few inches off the stock of the 8mm so it would fit into a mail sack, but the rifle was at my house when I arrived there. I shot many a Hampshire County deer with that rifle over the years.

39

We were quartered in civilian homes during our stay in Regensburg. Most of the houses were vacant because the civilians moved out when the War entered their neighborhood, and they didn't have the time or the means to move back. As we had at every other stop along the way, we found these homes warm and comfortable after weeks of sleeping on the ground in our bedrolls during the War.

Another assignment we had was delivering food and supplies to German civilians in the Regensburg area. With all means of transportation and manufacture obliterated by the Allied push at the end of the War, these civilians were desperate for any food that we could provide for them. We took our 2½-ton trucks to the one local bakery that was still operational each morning and crammed it full with these large, oval-shaped loaves of bread. The bread was so hard that we joked that if we dropped a loaf on the ground, it would shatter into a thousand pieces.

But the Germans would line up in droves to get that bread. There were no dairies still operating in the area, and cows were also in short supply, so they had no butter to put on their bread when they ate it. Instead, they would smear lard on the bread to give it some taste and extra nourishment. I was raised on a farm, and I'd often seen my mother cook with lard, but I'd never seen it eaten on bread. Those were desperate times for the German citizens, and even that type of nourishment was better than none at all, I suppose.

It's hard to imagine the suffering and misery the German people had to endure after the War. They had no homes, no clothes, and no food. I especially felt sorry for the little children, who ran through the streets in their ragged clothes with no shoes on their feet, their little faces streaked with dirt. They only had the U.S. Army to rely on for help, and I felt somewhat better when we delivered the bread to them each morning, even though I knew it was only small comfort in their suffering.

Those living in the country were somewhat better off because they at least had a few animals that they had been able to save from the German army, so they had some access to food. But the civilians living in the bigger cities were trapped, with no place to go and no way to get there if they had a place to go for help. Once more I hated the Nazis for the pain and suffering they had inflicted on their own people.

We had a chance to travel through the countryside when we moved from town to town, changing assignments. The German landscape reminded me very much of my home in West Virginia. There were rolling hills and open fields suited for farming. Each farm house had a barn that was so close to it that it almost seemed that the two were attached. I guess they liked having their precious animals close enough that they could keep a watchful eye on them at all times. I imagine the smell wasn't too pleasant, but at least they had the comfort of knowing that their livestock was safe from predators.

When it came to farm work, the women labored right alongside the men in the fields. In many cases, these frauleins were every bit as strong or stronger than the men. I remember passing one field where a farmer and his wife were loading sticks of firewood onto a wagon. These small logs were perhaps ten feet long and six inches wide at the bigger end. I saw one man and woman lugging a log across the field, and when they reached the wagon, the woman tossed her end aboard. The man was struggling with his load, and his wife walked up to him, grabbed the log from his hands, and tossed it casually onto the wagon. He had to be embarrassed, especially when the catcalls and laughter from everyone on our truck reached his ears.

Even in the country food was of the utmost importance, so often two or three families would go together and plant community gardens. These country folks had no farm machinery and few animals left after the War, so they cultivated their gardens by hand. They used a shovel called a spade to break up the ground for planting.

A spade was a small shovel that had a square blade that was perhaps six or eight inches wide. The blade was sharpened on the end, and the people would push the blade into the ground and turn over the soil one shovel full at a time. We would see twenty or thirty people lined up in a row, laboring over one patch of ground with those spades. It was backbreaking work, but those were desperate times that called for hard work if they were to survive.

40

As we moved south through Germany, fixing up roads and bridges along the way, we had a chance to visit Dachau, one of the Nazi death camps where thousands of Jews were killed during the War. We had heard stories about these death camps, where any Jew or other undesirable who couldn't be of use to the Third Reich was killed upon arrival, but I don't think I really believed that they existed until we saw Dachau.

The barbed wire that had surrounded the camp had been removed, and most of the barracks that housed the few Jews, who were useful enough to be worked to death by the Nazis, had been torn down. Such an eerie feeling overcame us when we entered the camp. It almost felt like the spirits of all those murdered there were still roaming around, and the stench from recently burned bodies still hung in the air.

I saw the arch over the entrance that read, "Arbeit macht frei" (Work sets you free), and I had to wonder what type of people would commit these atrocities against other human beings. Even though the War was over and my feelings toward the Nazis should have softened some, I still hated them for starting the War and for all the horrible things they had done to the people of Europe and their own citizens.

It's hard to describe the feelings that I carried with me during this time after the armistice. The War was over, but still anxiety and tension hung like a cloud over us all. We carried our weapons with us everywhere we went because we never knew when we would run into a bunch of SS troops or other Nazis who felt that the War really wasn't over and their duty still remained to kill as many Americans as they could.

That old axiom that we had been taught way back in Basic Training, "In war, you either kill or be killed," still very much applied. I couldn't understand the mentality that caused these fanatics to continue to kill people. Killing someone while defending one's country was one thing, but ambushing unsuspecting soldiers long after the War had ended was quite another.

To this day I don't understand the reasoning that led the Nazis to start the War, and I can't comprehend the mentality that led them to murder soldiers after peace had been declared. All I knew at the time was that we were helping the German people recover from a war that their own government had initiated, and those same people that we were trying to help were shooting at us. Somehow that scenario didn't make sense.

Losing comrades during the War was hard to accept, but someone being senselessly murdered after the War was over seemed like a tragic waste of life to me. I just tried to keep my eyes wide open, my head down, and my weapon at the ready at all times in an effort to ensure that I wasn't the next victim.

41

Maybe it was because I spent most of my time in Europe under his command, but one of the men that I most admired during the War was General Patton. He had a style and a flair about him that made men want to follow and fight for him. Even with all the flaws that sometimes cropped up in his personality, I still felt that our job in Europe would have been much tougher had we not had General Patton on our side. He was one of the truly great warriors of our or any other time.

One of our stops when traveling through Germany was the city of Heidelberg. Located in the southwest portion of Germany, Heidelberg had been devastated by Allied bombing, especially the roads leading to and from the city. We were sent there to try to make those roads passable.

Each morning we would pass the cottage that General Patton had commandeered for his post-War quarters. It was a small house with a broad lawn stretching down to the highway. On several occasions we would see General Patton out on the lawn taking his morning walk or just admiring the beautiful scenery. He cut such an imposing figure, standing there with his feet apart, his chest thrown out, and those ivory-handled pistols gleaming in the sunlight. He happened to be down close to the road as we passed one morning, and I got such a thrill when he returned my salute as we sped past.

We were working on a road repair job one morning in early December, and we had the radio on, as we almost always did on the job. A news flash came across the airwaves stating that General Patton had been involved in a traffic accident, but it gave no details as to his condition. As luck would have it, the accident was just a few miles from where we were working, so we piled into the truck and drove down there to see if we could get a close look.

By the time we arrived on the scene, the Army had thrown up a tight security ring around the crossroads. We did manage to get close enough to see the two vehicles involved in the accident, and we really didn't think that anyone was seriously hurt because the general's car had just minor damage to the front end. We really couldn't see much from so far away, but I do remember seeing the stars on the plate on the front of the general's Cadillac, which signified that the general had been riding in that vehicle. After an hour or so, we thought that we had better get back to work, and we left, not knowing how serious the wreck had been.

We learned later that General Patton and another officer were going on a hunting trip on the morning of the mishap. An Army truck delivering supplies had entered an intersection just before the general's car, and his driver hadn't seen the truck in time to avoid a collision. Neither vehicle was going very fast, and the accident seemed minor at first. The driver and the other passenger escaped unhurt, but General Patton didn't see the collision coming and was unprepared for the sudden jolt. He was thrown forward and struck his head on a piece of metal on the side of the car. His neck was broken on impact, and he was paralyzed from the neck down. He survived in a hospital for twelve days before passing away peacefully in the afternoon on December 21, 1945.

General Patton was known for taking risks while in command of his troops. He often intentionally exposed himself to enemy fire in the heat of battle to reassure and inspire his men. Many times he escaped extremely dangerous situations, and his men started to think that he was invincible. And suddenly, after the War was over and he was going out with a friend for a day of relaxation, he was killed.

As per his wishes before he died, General Patton was buried with his men in the Luxembourg American Cemetery near the city of Hamm. It seemed like such a waste of a brilliant military mind, and to echo his words to his wife just before his passing, "This is a hell of a way to die." I'm sure he would have much preferred to go in battle while leading his men, but one thing we can't and don't want to choose is when or how we will die. It was a sad day not only for those in his Third Army, but for freedom-loving people everywhere when the general passed so suddenly.

Days had quickly turned into months, and soon another Christmas and New Year had passed. We continued to move around Germany on various fix-up jobs, and the time seemed to pass quicker than I had feared it would when I found out right after the War how many points I still needed to go home.

Early in 1946, my company was transferred north to the city of Nuremberg to work on repairs to the Nuremberg Hotel, the largest hotel in the city. When we arrived there, the city looked like a landscape from the moon. We were told that over 90 percent of the city had been destroyed by Allied bombing and street fighting, and one look at the place told us that those estimates of damage were probably too low.

Nearly every building lay in ruins. Streets were blocked with debris, and random piles of rubble were everywhere. Of all the places we had seen after the War, Nuremberg was the most devastated. But somehow, this elegant old hotel that we had come to repair had at least retained some of its structural integrity.

An Allied bomb had fallen straight through the middle of the hotel and exploded on the ground floor. The center of the building was obliterated, but many of the rooms on the two wings were still standing and fairly strong. Our job was to rebuild the central part of the hotel and make it livable for American and other Allied officials who were there for the Nuremberg Trials.

The idea for this tribunal had been formed way back in April of 1945, before the War ended, and representatives from the four major Allied powers, the United States, Great Britain, France, and Russia, were selected as the lawyers and judges for the trials. Twenty-one of the most famous Nazi leaders from the War were tried in the first phase of the proceedings, which began on November 20, 1945.

The Allies wanted the trials to be held on German soil in a German courthouse, but Allied bombs had destroyed nearly all the courthouses in the major cities.

Even though Nuremberg was one of the most heavily damaged cities in the land, somehow its courthouse had survived.

It seemed ironic to me that the trials were conducted in Nuremberg, because that city had been the scene of massive Nazi rallies that attracted hundreds of thousands of people during the 1930's. It was also the site where the Nuremberg Laws were passed in 1935, which were regulations that stripped the Jews of nearly all their rights as German citizens and forbid Jews from associating with Aryan Germans in any way. Now some of the men who played integral roles in the passage of those regulations would be on trial for their lives in the very city where the laws were passed.

Each morning we would go to the prison compound and pick up German prisoners to help with the work on the hotel. These men were good workers, and we started to see progress on the repairs in just a few weeks. We worked five days a week, and on the weekends we were free to explore what was left of the city and the surrounding countryside. We worked on the hotel through the summer and fall, and near the middle of October of 1946, I got another rare opportunity to see history up close and personal.

Somehow our company commander was able to get passes for me and a buddy to attend the Nuremberg Trials for a day. I've never seen security as tight as it was around that courthouse. Not only were there armed guards lined all around the perimeter of the compound, but we also had to pass through six separate security checkpoints before we were allowed access to the courtroom. I guess the Army didn't want any radical SS troops barging in and shooting up the place.

Our seats were in a balcony that directly over-looked the witness stand, and the usher handed us a set of headphones before we sat down. We plugged in the phones, and we had a choice of five different languages we could listen to while following the proceedings. The lawyers and witnesses and judges would speak in their native tongues, and interpreters would translate what was said through the headphones.

When we sat down I immediately recognized the witness on the stand. It was none other than Hermann Goering, second in command to Hitler himself. Goering had been captured on May 8, 1945, in Austria by the U.S. Army, and, along with Rudolph Hess and Karl Doenitz, was one of the few Nazis who opted for surrender rather than death. We heard that he felt he was above prosecution because he was such an important world figure, but everyone knew that he had given many of the orders that led to the heinous crimes that the loyal Nazis had committed.

If he was above prosecution, apparently the lawyer who was grilling him on the stand hadn't gotten the memo. He badgered the German leader about specific orders that he had given and about war crimes that he had either initiated or been a party to. Goering, who looked like just a shell of the robust, portly man of his Nazi glory days, squirmed in his chair and repeatedly told the court that he either hadn't seen or been responsible for the actions mentioned in the questions, or he tried to explain them away as being natural consequences of war. He looked stunned and all alone, and if I hadn't known what a monster he had been over the years, I would almost have felt sorry for him.

I learned a few days after we saw him on the stand that Goering was found guilty of several war crimes and sentenced to death. Rather than suffer the humiliation of a public execution, Goering opted to take a cyanide capsule and commit suicide, just as his Fuehrer had done. It seemed that a brave, brilliant man like Goering, who could have done so much good in the world, had just wasted his life pursuing false beliefs and individual glory. But such was the case with many of those in the Nazi movement.

42

Work continued on the Nuremberg Hotel, and as time wore on I got to know some of the German prisoners who were helping with the repairs. There was one man who spoke fluent English, and he became the leader of our work gang because he could communicate with both the Americans and the other prisoners.

I was the man assigned to go to the detainment compound and pick up the work crew each morning in our truck. At this time we were employing about a dozen prisoners at the hotel. When we finished our work for the morning, I had one of the men in my squad take the prisoners to a room in the basement where they could eat the lunch that they brought with them from the compound. There was just the one door and no windows in the room, and the guard padlocked the prisoners inside and stood by the door until it was time to let them out for their afternoon work.

We often went to a local restaurant to eat our lunch, except for the unfortunate man who drew guard duty. I recall one afternoon when we entered the restaurant and encountered a large crowd of men near the door. When we finally waded through the throng and got to our table, we noticed that most of the attention was focused on one man near the back.

He was working his way toward the front, and as he passed our table I came face to face with none other than Mickey Rooney, the famous comedian and actor. He was there with the USO, and he couldn't have been nicer. He stopped at our table and shook everyone's hand. He even made small talk with us for a few minutes, asking us where we were from and how long we thought it would be before we got to go home. He may have been a big star in Hollywood, but he was just another Joe when he sat at the table and talked to us.

Lunch generally went off without a hitch, but one day in particular trouble reared its ugly head in a most unusual way. When lunchtime was over on this occasion, the guard unlocked the door and found one prisoner missing. He reported back to me, and I asked him how in the world anyone could have escaped. He was a reliable man, and I believed him when he told me that he had been vigilant in his guard duty and hadn't left the door for even a second. He had thoroughly searched the room before he left, and he could offer no explanation as to how that one man could have gotten away.

The prisoner who spoke fluent English ambled up to me and said that we had overlooked one possible escape route. He said that the room contained a bathroom at one time, and the missing man escaped by crawling through the sewer pipe that was located in the far corner of the room. I told him he was crazy, but I decided that I'd better go take a look just to see if it was possible.

When I got back down to the room, sure enough there was a sewer opening in the corner, just as my informant had said. But the opening couldn't have been more than ten or twelve inches in diameter. We went outside and traced the path of the pipe and found that it surfaced some three hundred feet from the building. The man who escaped was thin, but for him to be able to squeeze inside and then crawl through that pipe through who knows what kind of disgusting slime for that far seemed highly unlikely to me. But my informant insisted that was the case. For all we knew, that poor man suffered a horrible death from suffocation somewhere inside that sewer pipe.

Since I picked the prisoners up each morning, I was pretty sure that this escape meant trouble for me. If I took twelve prisoners in the morning, I was expected to return twelve prisoners that afternoon. We finished our day's work, and as we were returning to the prison compound a real sense of dread began to come over me. The major who was in charge of the compound wasn't one of my favorite people in the world anyway, and I could just imagine the hoops he would make me jump through because of my lapse in supervision. Even though we were no longer officially at war, losing a prisoner who could potentially take up arms and kill Allied soldiers was no minor mistake.

I decided that it was best to face the music, so after we returned the other prisoners I reported to the major's office and told him that I had lost a prisoner. This major was a real authority freak, the type of man who carried an extremely high opinion of himself, and he seemed to revel in the knowledge that he could impose his authority on someone. He asked how, if we had followed proper procedures, a prisoner could escape. I told him about the sewer pipe, and he just stared at me incredulously, as if to ask if I really expected him to believe such a wild tale.

After an awkward pause during which the major sat and sneered at me for several seconds, he told me that since I had lost a prisoner he had the authority to put me in prison to serve the rest of that man's time. I started to get scared because I couldn't tell if he was serious or not. I asked him if he would really do that to me. He sensed my fear, which made him adopt even more of a superior attitude, and he stated that he thought that was exactly what he was going to do.

I had no idea how long the man's sentence would run, and I also had no clue how I would explain to my parents that, although I had earned enough points to come home, I had to remain in prison in Germany until I served out that prisoner's sentence. I have to tell you that I was more than a little nervous about the situation.

I couldn't think of anything else to say, so I told him that he would have to talk to my company commander about this whole ordeal. I could only hope that he would be able to come up with some solution to my dilemma. The major replied that he would gladly speak to my commander. In fact, he said he couldn't wait to ream him out about the total lack of discipline the men under his command had shown that allowed such a lapse in judgment to occur.

I returned to headquarters and told the captain the whole story, including the major's threat to throw me in the stockade in the escaped prisoner's place. The captain said he would handle it the next morning and dismissed me. I spent a lonely, nervous night thinking about spending several weeks, months, or even years behind bars. After all, how could my commander, who was only a captain, override the wishes and orders of a major?

I was sweating bullets the next morning when the captain and I walked into the major's office. The major still had that same self-assured sneer on his face that he had when I left the day before. Apparently he hadn't listened to his mother about making faces, and his expression had actually frozen that way permanently. But as soon as I heard my captain speak, I felt much better.

Like facing down a bully on the playground, the captain told that major in no uncertain terms that he wasn't about to put one of his men in jail. He said that after all the Allied soldiers had gone through to win the War, the sacrifices they had made and the suffering they had endured, the major was out of his mind if he thought he would stand by and watch one of his men go to jail. He told the major that, although he was in command of the prison, he didn't run the captain's outfit, and if the major had anything else to say about the matter that he could take it up the chain of command. With that, the captain wheeled and marched out of the office, with me hot on his heels.

Leadership like that was hard to come by. The ultimate tribute to a soldier was when his commander stood up for him in the face of adversity. I loved my captain for sticking by me, and I would have done anything that he asked. I spent a couple more uneasy days waiting to see what would happen next, but I never heard anything else about the incident. I just hope that the prisoner got away. I would hate to think that I went through all that misery for a man who suffocated in a sewer pipe.

43

I mentioned before that my life fell into a routine very much like my civilian days. We worked five days a week on the hotel, but the weekends were pretty much our own. One of the main diversions for the American soldiers was gambling. The men played cards and rolled dice, and often hundreds or even thousands of dollars were riding on each hand or throw of the dice.

I wasn't much of a gambler because I always thought that my money was too hard to earn to risk losing it all to chance. I guess my caution came from a gene I inherited from Homer See. But every once in a while I would succumb to the temptation and join the others in a game of chance.

I recall one night when Lady Luck certainly smiled on me. I got involved in a dice game, and when I got control of those bones they turned to magic in my hands. Every time I rolled I either hit seven or eleven, or I made the point. I was so wrapped up in my sudden good fortune that I didn't realize that the men in the game were starting to drift away because all their funds had been lost. The last of the bettors finally left the ring, and I raked in what money was left in the middle.

I counted my small fortune and found I'd won over $500. I knew if I held on to the money that I would likely try to test my luck the next night, just to see if the magic was still there. And I also realized that the magic likely wouldn't be there two nights in a row, and my small fortune would be gone. I purchased a money order the next morning and mailed it home to my parents. I'm sure they were surprised to receive such a large sum of money, and I'm also sure that my mother wouldn't have approved of where it came from. I don't think I ever told her that I won the dough in a dice game.

While we were stationed in Nuremberg, we were quartered in an apartment building in a suburb called Furth. There were about fifty or sixty rooms in the apartment complex, and the accommodations were fairly nice. The rooms were pretty small, but each one was big enough for a bed and a dresser, and they all had individual bathrooms, which was particularly nice. I often marveled at how soft we had become in the few months since the War ended. We complained when the German in charge of the complex didn't fix up the coal furnace and our rooms would be freezing in the morning. Another pet peeve was cold showers. If the caretaker didn't fire the furnace, then there was no hot water.

Just a few months before, we had gone as many as thirty days on the line between showers. Our clothes were so filthy and smelly that we just threw them away when we finally did get off the line and get a shower. We stripped off our dirty clothes as we entered the showers and received new, clean clothes when we left the showers. We usually returned to the front in trucks that were open in the back, and the dust from unpaved roads seemed to be drawn into the back of those trucks. By the time we were back at the front, our clothes were nearly as dirty as they had been when we left. But at least we had the satisfaction of being clean for a little while.

While on the line, we washed and shaved with icy water that we poured into our helmets. We went to the bathroom behind the nearest tree. We ate cold rations and often stood watch and slept in foxholes that were half full of water or snow. I griped and moaned like the other soldiers, but deep down I was thankful to have a roof over my head, running water, and a secure place to sleep where I was pretty confident that nobody would take a shot at me.

There was a small dance hall just a short walk from our quarters, and every Saturday night the Army would organize a dance to entertain the troops. The local German women learned what time the dance started and what time most of the soldiers would be leaving to go there, and they lined up outside our door, waiting for a man to come by and notice them. They had a real fascination with American men, and many soldiers found their wives among those pretty young ladies who lined the sidewalk outside our quarters each Saturday night.

The man in charge of the dance hall was a small, wiry sergeant that the brass selected for just that service. He was in charge of cleaning and caring for the hall and maintaining order while the dances and other functions were going on. When I first saw him, I wondered why the Army selected such a little man for that big job, but once I saw him in action I understood.

As you might imagine, the beer and other alcoholic beverages flowed freely at those dances, and soldiers who had been used to combat needed only the slightest provocation to start a fight, especially when they had been drinking. I remember many a time when that little sergeant would wade right into the middle of a melee and break it up. He always seemed to know who the instigators were, and once he separated them, the others usually lost interest. But one Saturday night I thought for sure that he had met his match. Paratroopers were some of the meanest and toughest fighters in the U.S. Army. They were nasty when they were sober, but they were particularly mean when intoxicated. A soldier from the 101st Airborne wandered into the middle of a dance one Saturday wielding a pistol, and he vowed that he was going to shoot up the place. That paratrooper was a big, burly man, and we soon became convinced that he meant what he said. The dancers scattered to the far corners of the room, and nobody seemed to know exactly what to do.

Up stepped the little caretaker. He talked to the paratrooper and told him that he most certainly was not going to use that weapon. When the caretaker got near enough, he grabbed the bigger man in some sort of wrestling hold and forced him to the floor. In a matter of seconds, the caretaker disarmed the man and sent him on his way, telling the bigger man that he better never see him in that dance hall again. I'm not sure if he could have manhandled that big man had he not been drunk, but still we were amazed at the skill and courage of the littler sergeant. Fights seemed to be much less frequent after that incident.

Sundays were usually days of rest. Sometimes we would take short trips into the country to see the beautiful scenery or visit another town that was close by, but most of the time I would just lie around the barracks and relax in my room. I confiscated a German aviator helmet that was made of leather and had headphones built right into the sides. We had a big console radio in the lobby of our dormitory that we all enjoyed listening to, and some of the men in our company who were really good with electronics ran wires from that radio to all the rooms in the barracks. All I had to do was plug the wire into the receptacle on the aviator helmet, and I had stereo music playing right in my ears. I spent countless hours in my room relaxing on the bed as I listened to that sweet music.

The First and Seventh Armies both fielded baseball teams that were comprised of Major League players who enlisted in the Army during the War. These teams traveled around Europe after the War and played exhibition games against one another. One summer afternoon they came to Nuremberg to play in the huge stadium where Hitler held his Nazi party rallies in the 1930's. My whole platoon went to the game, and it was a real treat.

Several Major Leaguers played that day, but the one I remember the most was Ewell Blackwell. At 6'6" and 195 pounds, Blackwell earned the nickname "The Whip" shortly after his Major League debut for the Cincinnati Reds during the 1942 season. He pitched with a sidearm delivery that looked like he was throwing the ball from somewhere around third base. Even my untrained eye could easily see that Blackwell was destined for stardom. Had not arm miseries slowed him down, he would surely have ended up in the Baseball Hall of Fame.

Future Hall of Famer Roy Campanella caught Blackwell that day, and I recall that several other big name players were on the field. Because of my obligations on the farm, I didn't have the opportunity to play sports when I was growing up, and I'd certainly never attended a Major League game before, so it was a real thrill to watch those two teams, which were filled with some of the greatest baseball players in the world, battle it out on the field for Army pride. It was almost like watching the Major League All-Star Game in person.

44

Once the War ended, the Army started arranging leave for the soldiers who remained in Germany. The leave afforded us the opportunity to get away from our work and the devastation we saw each day on the job, and we also visited places that we would never otherwise get a chance to see. While I was stationed in Nuremberg, I was fortunate enough to be called for that leave.

Our leave was a two-week, all-expenses-paid trip to the breathtakingly beautiful country of Switzerland. We boarded a coal-fired steam engine train at the station in Nuremberg early in the morning for the first leg of our trip, and we switched to an electric train at the Swiss border because stem engines were not allowed in the country. Later that same night we arrived in Berne, the capital of Switzerland.

I thought I had seen mountains in West Virginia, but they turned out to be just hills compared to the majestic peaks that we encountered in Switzerland. I couldn't at the time, and still can't today, come up with the words to describe the beauty of the Swiss Alps. We were there in the fall of the year, but we could tell that winter was just around the corner. Ski season was in full swing, and the five-star hotel where we stayed was full of tourists from all over the globe.

There were high rollers from the United States there, some of whom had moved to the country permanently, not only because of the awesome natural beauty and tranquility but also because the cost of living was so much cheaper. Our first evening there we ate supper with an elderly couple originally from America who had just recently moved to Switzerland. The man, who was a retired CEO from some big corporation in the U.S., told me that he was never moving back to the States.

He said that he was staying at that expensive hotel for a fraction of what the same accommodations would cost him elsewhere, especially in the United States. He asked if I had any money to invest (a laughable thought to me at the time), and he said that property was so cheap in Switzerland that he could make me a small fortune in just a matter of a few years.

I felt really important when I ordered the same dishes from the menu that the millionaire and his wife were having. And the food there was excellent. We always had an appetizer, usually some type of soup, before each meal, and the main course was delicious. We feasted the entire two weeks that we were there, all at the Army's expense. I couldn't help but think that just a few short months ago I had been freezing my butt off in a foxhole with nothing but K Rations to eat. This old farm boy from Rada sure had come a long way!

Switzerland declared itself to be a neutral country in the War, but Hitler had taken over the government and inflicted some minor damage in the process. But by the time we arrived there late in the fall of 1945, there were few or no reminders that the Swiss had ever been in the vicinity of the War. That was the neatest, cleanest country that I have ever encountered. There were few factories there, so the air was always fresh and crisp. It seemed that not one blade of grass was out of place. For a country boy like me, this was as near to Heaven as I had ever been.

Outdoor sports were all the rage in Switzerland. Bern had several outdoor ice-skating rinks at various points around the city, and it was there that I learned to skate. I'd slipped and slid around on the ice on farm ponds and on Patterson Creek, but I'd never actually been on skates before that trip. When we got to the rink, I was amazed to see skaters of all ages whizzing past me. I especially enjoyed watching the little kids, some of whom couldn't have been more than two or three, as they glided gracefully around the rink. I took several spills before I got the hang of skating, but by the end of my stay I could almost keep up with the very young and the elderly on skates.

No trip to the Alps would be complete without trying skiing. Once more I was amazed at the skill and grace the Swiss exhibited as they swooshed down the slopes. I thought skating was hard to master, but it couldn't hold a candle to the skills necessary to master skiing. After just the briefest of lessons at the bottom of the slopes, we boarded the chair lift for the breathtaking trip to the top.

I literally gawked around with my mouth agape, looking at the natural beauty surrounding me as the lift slowly moved toward the top of the mountain. However, I soon found that the scenery and the slopes were much more enjoyable from the lift than they were from the ground.

The second I slid off the lift I knew I was in serious trouble. I just couldn't make those skis do what I wanted them to do. One ski wanted to go left while the other headed off to the right. Just staying upright for a few feet was a major accomplishment. I fell so many times that I feared I would never get to the bottom. I could just envision the rescue party, complete with a big St. Bernard dog, finding me several days later, stuck in a snowdrift halfway down the slope.

I finally surrendered and just sat down where my last spill had occurred. The instructor had to ride the lift back to the top, ski down to where I was stranded, take my skis off, and help me walk the rest of the way down the hill. The scenery was really beautiful on the slopes, but I'm not sure enough money had been printed to make me try skiing again.

We took several day trips to other cities, including Zurich. Everything about the country and its people fascinated me. We rode on an apparatus that they called an incline, and I have to admit that it was the oddest form of transportation that I had ever seen. It had a car that was all glass in front and very much resembled an elevator. The incline ran on tracks that went right up the face of a mountain that was at least 2,000 feet tall. As the car crawled up the mountain, the scenery was even more beautiful than from the ski lift. I once more was in awe of the natural splendor that spread out before me.

The weirdest part of the incline was that it operated on water power. Each car had a water tank on the bottom that had to hold several hundred gallons.

There were two cars that ran on tracks side-by-side, one going up as the other went down. A large cable that wrapped around a giant pulley at the top of the mountain regulated the movement of the cars.

When passengers had been loaded on each end, water was pumped into the car at the top of the mountain. The added weight of the water started that car down the mountain while pulling the other car toward the top. When all the passengers were loaded once more, the water was pumped out of the car at the bottom while the tank on the car at the top was filling up. The difference in the weight of the water moved the cars up and down. It was a concept that I hadn't seen before, and I was fascinated by it. We must have ridden that incline a dozen times, each trip just as exciting as the one before. I felt like a kid taking his first ride on a Ferris wheel.

The only sore spot about the trip actually occurred when I reached the border entering the country. Many soldiers had either bought or confiscated mechanical drawing sets during their travels around Germany. Engineers and architects used the instruments in those sets to draw up plans for buildings and bridges. The soldiers found out that the Swiss coveted these instruments, so they would haul the sets with them when they went to Switzerland on leave and sell or trade them for all types of expensive items, especially jewelry and world famous Swiss watches.

When one of my friends found out that I was going on leave in Switzerland, he asked if I would take his drawing set with me and see if I could trade it for a watch. I reluctantly agreed to the arrangement, although I can't say that I was overly enthusiastic about it. As I stowed the drawing set in the bottom of my travel bag, I just had a feeling that something would go wrong, and my fears were confirmed at the border.

When we reached the train station on the Swiss border where we were to load onto the electric train for the rest of our trip, they herded all of us passengers into a room in the station and told us to take everything out of our bags. Apparently German merchandise, especially the drawing sets, was fetching quite a price in Switzerland. It had become such an economic problem that the government had closed their border to all items from Germany that the thousands of GI's who were visiting Switzerland were transporting into the country.

I had never been told about this new regulation, so when the border guard looked through my belongings he immediately asked why I would have these tools in my possession, since I obviously was neither an architect nor an engineer. I told him the truth. I said that a buddy of mine gave me the set to trade for a watch. The guard said in no uncertain terms that I certainly wasn't going to do any such thing. He said that his government had granted him the authority to confiscate all such items, and that was what he was going to do. He also said that my commanding officer would be getting a call to tell him what had happened.

I panicked. I had no idea how my friend would react when I told him that I had lost his drawing set. I also had no clue how my commanding officer would feel when he found out that I had tried to illegally smuggle this contraband into Switzerland. I tried to talk the guard out of taking the set by telling him that I promised not to trade or sell it while I was in Switzerland. He was unmoved, but I finally convinced him to hold the set for me until I returned from leave. However, he said that he had to call my commanding officer, or he could lose his job.

I was sure that he would not be around when I returned, but I must have run into the one honest border guard at that checkpoint. When I came through on my way back to Germany, he was there to return the drawing set. I felt better when I got the tools back, but I still had to face my commanding officer.

Captain McCormick, who had been my company commander since way back in England, was a fair man who always stood up for his men, but I was still pretty nervous when he called me into his office the day after I returned from leave. He asked what I was doing with the drawing set, and I told him the truth, that a buddy had given it to me to trade for a watch.

The captain said that his superiors required him to hand out some sort of discipline for the infraction, and that some men had been busted all the way back to a private for that offense. I stammered and told him that sounded pretty rough. I could only think that I had carried a spotless military record throughout my time in the Service only to be busted from a sergeant to a private for doing a friend a favor this close to the end. What would my mother think when she found out?

He stopped and thought for a few agonizing seconds, and then a small smile crossed his face. He winked and said that he would put on paper that he had confined me to quarters for two weekends, which should satisfy his superiors, but that he would trust me to keep the fact that I hadn't really served the sentence between the two of us. I told him that was a secret that I would gladly keep. Just as when he stood up for me in front of the major who had threatened to throw me in the brig to finish the German prisoner's sentence, I was eternally grateful to Captain McCormick for the compassion and understanding he showed to me. I guess keeping my mouth shut and doing my job well had finally paid off.

The two weeks of leave passed much too quickly, but I'll cling to the memories of that trip for as long as I live. I hated the War and the destruction that it spread all over the world, but were it not for the War, I wouldn't have had the opportunity to travel to Switzerland and visit that fairy tale land. I guess in that regard I was lucky to serve in the U.S. Army and fight for my country.

45

Work continued for several more weeks on the Nuremberg Hotel until we got it to the point where guests could actually stay there without worrying whether the roof would fall in on them in the middle of the night. When those repairs were completed, my company was transferred to a town called Regensburg to work on repairing the roads and bridges in that vicinity.

The weather was still frigid as the calendar turned from January to February. The way I figured my points, I still had several months of duty to complete in Germany before I could even start to think about heading home. I really didn't think about it all that much, because I had a job that paid me a decent wage (96 dollars a month, up from 21 dollars a month when I first entered the Service), but I really didn't worry too much about the money because the Army was feeding and clothing me and providing a place for me to live. As I had in every other job that I'd had up to that point, I went to work every day, did my job, and went back home in the evening.

Groups of soldiers were leaving to go home every week, and I noticed that some of the men I had served with were now among those headed for the States. But I tried not to get too anxious about the situation, because I guess I didn't want to get my hopes up that I would be next only to have them dashed when my name didn't appear on the next list. In fact, in February of 1946 I really didn't know how many points I had accumulated. I suppose it goes back to that habit that country folks had about concentrating on what is directly in front of them and not worrying all that much about the future.

We were staying in a dormitory that had been an apartment complex before the War when we were stationed in Regensburg, and there was a big bulletin board out in front of the barracks where the Headquarters Company posted all the vital news of the day, like what the next movie would be and when the next big social event, like a dance, would be held. In one corner of that board they posted a list of all the men who would be included in the next wave going home. One morning in the middle of February, Buck See's name appeared on that list.

I'm still not sure how my points added up so fast, but believe me I was in no mood to ask any questions. I'd never disobeyed an order in the three years I'd been in the Military, and if the Army said it was time for me to go home, then I certainly wasn't going to disobey an order at that point.

I tried not to get too anxious about my departure, because the assigned day was still several days away, so I kept going to work and tried to put it out of my thoughts. But there were times, especially late at night when I had trouble sleeping, that my mind wandered to home and what my family was doing and how I would feel when I was a civilian again at last.

The days seemed to last forever, but finally the appointed time came, and I packed up my gear, said my good-byes to the members of my squad and company who were left behind, and headed for the train station. The troop train that we took leaving Germany was much more comfortable than the one we rode on coming into the country. It wasn't nearly as crowded, and we didn't have the threat of combat hanging over our heads. Even though the trip took two days, I really didn't mind it all that much. It felt more like we were traveling on a vacation rather than going to work, and that was a feeling I hadn't enjoyed for the past three years.

Cherbourg was bustling when we unloaded from the train early in the morning of March third and headed for our barracks for the night. All the souvenirs that I accumulated, like the 8mm rifle and the silver bayonet that I had confiscated from the SS colonel, had been mailed home in advance, because I knew that if I wanted to keep any mementos of the War I'd better not have them on me when I reported to the ship to head home.

Since we no longer had any use for it, we turned in all our gear that we had used in the field while we were in combat, including our bedrolls, our packs, our entrenching tools, and our weapons. All we were allowed to keep were our Army clothes. Before we boarded the ship to come home, we had to empty our duffel bags so the men on the docks could search through our belongings to make sure that we weren't bringing anything home that didn't belong to us.

I saw all kinds of valuables, from war souvenirs to jewelry and weapons and silverware, just about anything a soldier felt was memorable or valuable, thrown in huge piles along the dock. There were thousands of dollars' worth of possessions heaped up there. I often wondered what happened to all that stuff. Did the officers sort through it and take out what they wanted? It certainly wasn't returned to its original owners. I'll bet there are officers all over the United States with spare rooms filled with those valuables. But the common soldier, unless he was very crafty or knew the men searching his possessions, got very little of it. I guess that's just the way the Army, and the world for that matter, operates. The person that does most of the dirty work has to defer to those in authority when the time comes to divide the spoils.

Our ride back to the U.S. was far superior to the one we took over to Europe in just about every way. We rode on an American Navy cruiser that hauled approximately 1,400 soldiers, making it much less crowded. The ship was neat and clean, unlike the filthy conditions we endured on our voyage to England. It was nearly twice as fast as the British ship. We covered the distance back to America in just seven days. But by far the biggest difference was in the food.

I'm not sure whether I just looked like a chef, or whether I was just born lucky, but every time I was around a kitchen or galley, I drew KP duty. It happened on the ship going over to England, and it also happened on the Navy vessel coming home. I served KP duty three different times on the trip to the U.S., but this time there was a silver lining to this cloud of KP duty.

First of all, I wasn't ashamed to help serve the food and clean up the kitchen, because the meals that came out of that galley were first rate. We had meat and vegetables and bread, and all of it tasted really good. The best part, however, was the little bonus that the cooks gave to the men who helped them out.

On my first day on KP, the cooks came to me and said that they would be glad to fix any dish they had for the men who worked in the galley. Any time of day, all we had to do was make a request, and they would do their best to see that we got it. We ate steak, fish, and chicken almost on demand, and the food was delicious. I didn't mind putting a little elbow grease on those pots and pans when I knew that a meal specially prepared for me was waiting at the end of my shift. I can't say that I particularly enjoyed KP duty, but that food sure made it a lot more bearable.

Our sleeping quarters were much better on the Navy ship. Instead of the filthy hammocks that the German prisoners of war had slept in right before they became our beds, we had regular bunks that folded down from the wall. These bunks came in rows of four or five, and the linen on them was fresh and clean, at least when we started our trip.

The only aspect of the trip that the Navy couldn't control was the weather. About three days into our voyage we ran into some very rough seas. The ship rolled and rose and dipped and rocked until I was sure that the old bucket would come apart. I recall sitting at the supper table one evening in the middle of the storm. The ship was gyrating in all different directions to the point that the plates, glasses, and silverware were sliding from one end of the table to the other, and then back again. Nearly all the soldiers were either white from fright or green from seasickness.

The sailors went about their business as usual, as

though this type of weather was a common occurrence, which, I suppose, it was for those Navy veterans. One ensign just laughed at us and told us to wait until we ran into a real storm, and then we would really see something. If this was just a "little squall," as the sailors called it, I surely didn't want to go through a real storm.

My seasickness wasn't nearly as bad coming home as it had been going over to England. I think the quality of the food had something to do with it. Also, the voyage was only half as long, so the time I was sick was much shorter. I spent my share of time at the rail and in the john, especially during that "little squall," but overall I guess I started to get my sea legs and developed a little stronger stomach when it came to sailing on the high seas.

I mentioned before that gambling was a regular recreational outlet for many of the soldiers that served during the War. Men gambled on the boat going over to Europe; they gambled when they had a spare minute during the War; they really gambled to help pass the time after the War ended. But games of chance reached a whole new level on the boat back home.

Most of the soldiers on our ship hadn't seen their homes or their loved ones for three or four years. The idea of getting home and resuming their civilian lives made them happy and carefree. Also, we had a little money in our pockets, and some of us thought that gambling was the way to turn that little bit of money into a fortune. Such thinking is the basis of the lotteries that almost every state now sponsors.

I'm not sure those reasons adequately explain the crazy way that many men threw their money around on the voyage home, but the gambling, both cards and dice, started when the anchor was weighed in France and continued nearly nonstop for the entire seven days that we were on the boat. Some soldiers realized their dreams of huge winnings, but far more men left these games of chance with just the clothes on their backs.

I recall one crap game in particular. These two soldiers started the game while we were still in the port in France, and I'm not sure that they slept the entire seven days we were on the boat. I know when I finished my breakfast and wandered over to the game on our first day out, these two were already in full swing. The crap table was a large ring of at least thirty or forty men who surrounded one corner of our sleeping quarters. It sounded like the New York Stock Exchange as men yelled out their bets at the tops of their lungs and celebrated in their triumphs or wailed at their losses.

The two men running the game operated as a team. One man served as the banker, who fielded all bets and placed the appropriate amount of money in the middle of the ring to cover them all. The other member of the team was the roller, and I'd have to say that he was the luckiest man on the face of the Earth, or he was the best cheater that any of us had ever seen, depending on your perspective. All I know for sure is that he and his partner made not a small but a huge fortune from that game.

The object of the game of craps is to roll desired numbers with the dice on demand. If the roller tosses a seven or an eleven, he is an automatic winner. If he rolls another number (which oddly enough went by the name "point"), then he gets one more chance to roll that number again. If he makes the point (rolls that same number again), then he is also a winner. If the roller fails to roll a seven or an eleven and doesn't make the point, then the men around the circle are the winners. It's really a simple game, but often thousands of dollars rode on each roll of the dice. I've never seen anything like the luck that roller had. If he didn't roll a seven or eleven, he almost always made the point. Several of the men around the circle accused him of throwing loaded dice, which were dice that had been doctored to only land on certain numbers. The accusations became so loud and menacing that the roller finally told the other gamblers that he would throw any dice that they had. Someone would come up with a new set of dice, and the roller would continue his incredible run of luck.

It seemed like the roller won every single time the dice were rolled, which not only would have made me suspicious of his honesty but would also have taken most of the fun out of the game for me. The game was much too rich for my blood and my wallet, but I stood and watched in amazement as those two men cleaned out nearly everyone else on the ship. He won so often that he had to be cheating, but he changed dice many times and just kept on winning. If he was a cheater, then he was the best cheater at a game that I've ever run into.

The roller's partner stood on one side of the ring with a long wooden paddle in his hands. He threw enough money into the ring to cover all bets, and much more often than not he would rake in a huge pile of cash after each round. He howled and laughed and heckled the men into throwing more and more cash into the ring. Then he would howl and laugh all the louder as he raked in the next pile of money.

Most of us didn't have a lot of money, but some people had to be loaded because the supply of cash in the middle never ran dry. Many men had made big sums of money dealing on the black market after the War, selling food and supplies and cigarettes to the German people, but their ill-gotten gains didn't last very long if they entered that crap game. Those two had to have raked in hundreds of thousands of dollars over the seven-day trip. It truly was amazing.

46

Late in the afternoon of the seventh day of the trip, we pulled into New York Harbor. We cruised right past the Statue of Liberty, and the rivets on that old ship rattled at the roar the men on our boat lifted as we passed Lady Liberty. We hadn't seen the Statue on our way out to Europe because we left after dark, but the sun glistening off the Grand Old Lady brought a tear to all our eyes as we glided past her. We were really back in America at last!

We walked down the same gangplank we had walked up eighteen months before, and darkness had fallen before we picked up our gear and boarded the buses headed for Camp Kilmer, the spot where we spent our last night before heading off to England. After we stowed our gear in the barracks, we walked to the mess hall for dinner. As we filed into the mess hall, we had no clue what a treat we had in store.

The cooks told us to sit back and relax because they were serving our Army farewell meal. The meal would consist of a seventeen-course steak dinner complete with all the trimmings. We started with soup and a salad and then progressed to the main course, the most succulent T-bone steak I had ever tasted. We had potatoes and other vegetables and all the pastries and other desserts that we could cram into our mouths. I don't think I've ever been as full as I was that night when I crawled into bed at last.

Men were headed to points all over the country to be discharged. The Army tried to locate the fort or post closest to each man's home, and then all the travel arrangements, mostly by civilian buses or trains, needed to be completed. All told, we remained in Camp Kilmer for three days before all the connections and reservations were arranged.

Early the fourth morning of our return to American soil, we loaded on buses that took us to Grand Central Station in New York City. My destination was Fort Meade, Maryland, just outside Baltimore. We rode in luxury on the train, since much of the crunch on rail travel that had existed during the War had subsided somewhat.

We pulled into the station in Baltimore later that same afternoon, and an Army bus was waiting outside the station to take us to Fort Meade. After we ate another delicious meal, we walked over to a large warehouse to trade in our old clothes for a whole new set of uniforms.

The new uniforms had none of the patches or decorations on them, so after we received them we walked into a large sewing factory where our awards were added. German prisoners, who I assumed had been sent back home months before, were the ones sewing the patches on the uniforms. There were hundreds of sewing stations in the factory, and my patches were sewn on and my decorations attached in short order.

We were all so happy to be back on home soil, but as I watched these Germans working with their sewing machines I wondered what must have been going through their minds. I'm sure they all had families back in their native land, and some of them had been away for several years without seeing their loved ones. But here they were in a strange land where the people spoke a foreign language, and many of the customs were just as foreign.

The War had ended nearly a year before, and yet these men continued to be confined here in America. I'm not really sure how much longer they stayed in the United States, but their plight was much worse than ours when we served occupation duty in Germany. At least we had some leisure time when we could go out and blow off a little steam and enjoy our freedom. They were still prisoners in a foreign land. I tried to put myself in their places, which made me all the more grateful that our side had emerged victorious.

Before we boarded the bus for home, the Army gave each of us the back pay we had coming, plus a farewell bonus. I hadn't been paid in three months, which amounted to $288, and the $300 bonus brought my total to nearly $600. That may not sound like a lot of money by today's standards, but in 1946 I felt pretty good with that wad bulging in my pocket.

Late in the afternoon of March 13, 1946, the bus I was riding in pulled into the station in Cumberland, Maryland. I had called my sister Hazel before the bus left Fort Meade and told her what time I would arrive in Cumberland, and her smiling face greeted me as I walked down the steps. She had a million questions for me during the 45-minute ride home, and I just had to keep pinching myself to make sure that this whole thing wasn't a dream.

Hazel parked her car at the Rada Store, which she and her husband Bill were running at the time, and I threw my duffel bag over my shoulder and walked the 100 yards or so home. Mother was the first to greet me when I walked through the door. She screamed and cried and threw her arms around me as the other members of my family crowded around. They all jabbered on about how different I looked and how dashing I was in my brand new uniform.

As we chattered on about what had been going on in their lives and how I was feeling after finally getting home, my father emerged from the kitchen and walked toward me. The first thought that came to me was how much older he looked. I'm not sure if it was the strain of all the hard work on the farm or the worrying he had done over his son in the War, but he looked decades older to me, even though he was only 55 years old. I shook his hand, and he smiled and welcomed me home.

The greeting lasted for several minutes, with each of my siblings taking his or her turn telling me the latest family news, and my mind started to wander to all the things that had happened to me since I'd last been in that house. I left home a near invalid two and a half years before, suffering from an unknown disease that left me as suddenly and mysteriously as it had come upon me. I returned a man who had experienced the unspeakable horrors of war and somehow managed to escape without a scratch.

I was just twenty-two when I got back home, but I felt much older. I still had my whole life before me, but as of yet I really hadn't made too many plans. I was still just a common farm boy at heart, and all I could think about was my home and family, the things directly in front of me. All I knew for sure was that I was home at last, and that felt mighty good.

47

So there you have it. That's my father's story. And he was right. He still had a long life ahead of him, a life that has endured into its 88th year and counting. Less than a year after he returned from the Army he fell in love with and married my mother, a War widow who was struggling to raise three small children. The two of them blended her two sons and a daughter with three more boys of their own to form a strong, loving family of simple country folks that pretty much still focuses on the things right in front of them and lets tomorrow take care of itself when the time comes, just like my dad's family before us. But that's a different story for another time.

As I've started to age, I've come to realize what I think I knew all along. My father is a pretty smart man. He can fix practically anything, and his advice on everything from relationships to money to standing up for what you believe in has never steered me wrong.

But I've also come to realize that he can make mistakes at times. For instance, take the last paragraph of his story. He said that he hadn't thought all that much about his future because he was just a common farm boy. Wow, was he wrong on that assessment. It's been my experience over the 58 years of my life that Buck See may be the most uncommon man I've ever come across.

Larry See was raised in West Virginia and has remained a Mountaineer his entire life. A 1973 graduate of Hampshire High School in Romney, Larry attended Shepherd College, earning a BA in English and physical education in 1977. He returned to his native Hampshire County after graduation and taught in the public school system for the next 33 years. After retiring in 2010, he was employed by the Hampshire County Commission, serving as the Director of Parks and Recreation.

He is married to the former Donna Bazzle, and they have two children. Amy See Delaplain, 29, is an elementary teacher in Hampshire County, and Philip, age 26, is the West Virginia University 4-H Extension Agent in Boone County, West Virginia. They also have a foster son, Carlos McCormick, who currently attends Tennessee State University in Nashville.

An athlete in both high school and college, Larry coached a variety of sports on the scholastic level, most notably serving as the head basketball coach at his alma mater for 17 years. He and Donna remain active in sports and fitness.

The Sees are members of Romney First Baptist Church, where Larry serves as a Sunday School teacher and as a member of the Deacon Board.